Cambridge Elements ≡

Elements in the Philosophy of Religion
edited by
Yujin Nagasawa
University of Birmingham

RELIGIOUS DISAGREEMENT

Helen De Cruz
Oxford Brookes University

CAMBRIDGE
UNIVERSITY PRESS

CAMBRIDGE
UNIVERSITY PRESS

University Printing House, Cambridge CB2 8BS, United Kingdom

One Liberty Plaza, 20th Floor, New York, NY 10006, USA

477 Williamstown Road, Port Melbourne, VIC 3207, Australia

314–321, 3rd Floor, Plot 3, Splendor Forum, Jasola District Centre,
New Delhi – 110025, India

79 Anson Road, #06–04/06, Singapore 079906

Cambridge University Press is part of the University of Cambridge.

It furthers the University's mission by disseminating knowledge in the pursuit of
education, learning, and research at the highest international levels of excellence.

www.cambridge.org
Information on this title: www.cambridge.org/9781108457316
DOI: 10.1017/9781108557849

First published 2019

A catalogue record for this publication is available from the British Library.

ISBN 978-1-108-45731-6 Paperback
ISSN 2399-5165 (online)
ISSN 2515-9763 (print)

Cambridge University Press has no responsibility for the persistence or accuracy of
URLs for external or third-party internet websites referred to in this publication
and does not guarantee that any content on such websites is, or will remain,
accurate or appropriate.

Religious Disagreement

DOI: 10.1017/9781108557849
First published online: December 2018

Helen De Cruz
Oxford Brookes University

Abstract: This Element examines what we can learn from religious disagreement, focusing on disagreement with possible selves and former selves, the epistemic significance of religious agreement, the problem of disagreements between religious experts, and the significance of philosophy of religion. Helen De Cruz shows how religious beliefs of others constitute significant higher-order evidence. At the same time, she advises that we should not necessarily become agnostic about all religious matters, because our cognitive background colors the way we evaluate evidence. This allows us to maintain religious beliefs in many cases, while nevertheless taking the religious beliefs of others seriously.

Keywords: epistemology of disagreement, permissivism, uniqueness, conciliationism, religious belief

ISBNs: 9781108457316 (PB) 9781108557849 (OC)
ISSNs: 2399-5165 (online) 2515-9763 (print)

Contents

1 How Should We Respond to Religious Disagreement?

1.1 The Significance of Religious Disagreement

> In the midst of this war of words and tumult of opinions, I often said to myself:
> What is to be done? Who of all these parties are right; or, are they all wrong
> together? If any one of them be right, which is it, and how shall I know it?
>
> (Smith, 1902, 4)

Joseph Smith grew up in a religiously diverse community in New York
(Palmyra and Manchester) during the Second Great Awakening (about
1790–1850s). He came into contact with many religious (mainly Christian)
denominations, including Methodism, Presbyterianism, Baptism, but also with
folk religious magic, which was practiced in his family. The open disagreement
between these religious groups, which were trying to win converts, troubled
him. Whom should he trust?

> Presbyterians were most decided against the Baptists and Methodists, and
> used all the powers of both reason and sophistry to prove their errors, or, at
> least, to make the people think they were in error. On the other hand, the
> Baptists and Methodists in their turn were equally zealous in endeavoring to
> establish their own tenets and disprove all others. (Smith, 1902, 3–4)

The fifteen-year-old Smith solved this conundrum by retreating into the woods
and asking God for guidance. This eventually led to a series of visions, which in
turn led him to establish a new religious movement, the Church of Jesus Christ
of the Latter Day Saints (also known as Mormonism). Put in epistemological
terms, Smith's solution to the problem of religious disagreement was to try to
seek additional evidence, in his case, in the form of revelation.[1] This example
illustrates that religious disagreement constitutes some form of evidence. It is
a peculiar form of evidence, in that it does not directly bear on the truth or
falsity of religious beliefs, but rather on us as epistemic agents. When confronted with conflicting viewpoints, we sometimes try to gather more information, as in Smith's case. Disagreement is thus a form of *higher-order evidence.*
Higher-order evidence has a few peculiar features. For example, its value
seems to be dependent on who is evaluating it. If Kabita disagrees with Dan
about the epistemic credentials of Buddhism, then Kabita's beliefs are higher-
order evidence for Dan, but not for Kabita. It would indeed be a bit peculiar if
Kabita said, "I am a very thoughtful sort of person, and I am a Buddhist.
My belief must constitute some evidence for Buddhism!" She would be
hubristic, to say the least. But it is not at all unusual if Dan took Kabita's belief

---

[1] This account of Joseph Smith's "first vision" is canonical among Mormons, but it is somewhat
idealized. For a more nuanced account, see Taves (2016).

as some form of evidence, thinking along the following lines, "I know Kabita is a thoughtful sort of person. If she is a Buddhist, maybe Buddhist beliefs – about enlightenment, reincarnation, and the like – are not as outlandish as I thought they were. Maybe there is something I am missing." This asymmetry merely demonstrates that disagreement constitutes evidence that is relative to the agent, not that it would be irrelevant (Christensen, 2010; Matheson, 2009).

Joseph Smith's case also illustrates another feature of religious disagreement: recognizing its epistemic significance has a practical, real-world impact on the religious beliefs we hold. Once we see that people who are just as thoughtful and well informed as we are come to very different religious viewpoints, we can no longer go on taking our own religious views for granted. Nicholas Wolterstorff (1996) draws a distinction between analytic and regulative epistemology. Analytic epistemology, according to Roberts & Wood (2007, 20), aims to produce "theories of knowledge, rationality, warrant, justification, and so forth, and proceeds by attempting to define these terms." By contrast, regulative epistemology is a more practically oriented way of thinking about these concepts; it tries to provide guidance for how to shape our doxastic practices (Wolterstorff borrows the term "doxastic practice" from Alston [1991]). A doxastic practice is a system of habits by which we form our beliefs. Regulative epistemology proposes doxastic practices that help us acquire beliefs that are responsibly formed. They can, for instance, be aimed at obtaining as many true beliefs as we are able, or they can be more risk averse and help us avoid making mistakes. As James (1902) already noted, there is sometimes a tension between these two desired states of affairs (believing true things and avoiding believing false things), so a risk-seeking person might be more inclined to believe what is not certain, while a risk-averse person would avoid it.[2] Thus a doxastic practice needs to specify first what epistemic utility we would like to obtain, for example, obtaining true beliefs, avoiding false beliefs, or avoiding false beliefs of specific kinds. Once specified, it can help us obtain these utilities. Regulative epistemologies are often borne out of a concrete need, which is precipitated by a social and intellectual crisis (Wolterstorff, 1996). In the case of Descartes and Locke, this was the unraveling of the medieval Christian consensus in the seventeenth century. To provide a simplified picture of what happened, at the end of the Middle Ages the general consensus on moral and factual matters weakened as a result of several factors.

---

[2] See Pettigrew (2016) for a recent formal argument that vindicates James and that shows that it is rationally permissible for epistemic risk seekers to go significantly beyond the evidence and believe something for which they can never have incontrovertible evidence, such as the existence of the external world, of other minds, or of God.

These included the increasing recognition that there was a wide diversity of religious beliefs across the world, due to increasing contact with foreign cultures as a result of colonialism and trade. Reports of religious beliefs in other cultures were often secondhand, not systematically collected, and distorted. Nevertheless, they provided evidence that religious beliefs varied considerably, and that monotheism was not universal. As Hume (1757, 2) summarized it, "no two nations, and scarce any two men, have ever agreed precisely in the same sentiments."

As we will see in Section 4, observations like these weakened the argument from common consent for theistic belief, the argument that theism must be true because it is universal. Added to this was the growth of experimental science, which showed that many religious claims, such as about the age of the earth or the origin of species, were false. Further epistemic shifts occurred with the end of logical positivism in the middle of the twentieth century. Logical positivism sought new epistemic certainty by appeal to empirically verifiable statements. With its downfall, it became clear that scientific findings could not take on the role that formerly religious dogmas had played in the Middle Ages. Today, we may be experiencing another epistemic crisis, the increasing polarization and tribalization of beliefs, exacerbated by political echo chambers. For example, a study by Gauchat (2012) shows that from the 1970s onward, scientific beliefs have become increasingly politically polarized in the United States. Given this, what doxastic practices should we adopt? The aim of this Element is to be regulative, rather than analytic, even though it will use tools of analytic epistemology. I will not here attempt to make a comprehensive survey of religious disagreement in all its different forms. Rather, I will examine what practical conclusions we can draw in the face of particular forms of religious disagreement.

1.2 Conciliationism and Steadfastness

Let's for the moment assume that disagreement about religion has some evidential value (I will respond to some objections to this claim later in this section). Social epistemologists have been debating how we should respond to this evidence. Take this example, adapted from Clayton Littlejohn (2013):

> **Complacent atheist:** Clayton is a complacent atheist: he strongly believes there is plenty of evidence against the existence of God. However, he is also aware of the fact that there are several philosophers who believe in God. Many of these have thought carefully about the matter and are experts in epistemology, metaphysics, and other relevant philosophical subdisciplines.

Two broad lines of response are open to the complacent atheist. The first option falls under the umbrella of conciliationism. The conciliatory position[3] holds that we should revise our opinions, or become less confident of them, in the face of disagreement with someone we consider to be an epistemic peer about the subject matter. So if Clayton believes that, say, Linda (a theist philosopher) is just as thoughtful and epistemically virtuous as he is, and that she has access to the same body of evidence, he should revise his beliefs. Maybe he should suspend judgment on the issue entirely and become an agnostic, as Feldman (2007) recommends. If he does not wish to go this far, he should at least become less complacent in his atheism, say, move his credence[4] that atheism is true from .9 to .7 (depending on whether he believes he should lend equal weight to Linda's views).

A second option is to remain steadfast, and not change one's credences at all. There are several motivations for remaining steadfast, which may apply in a religious context. For example, Wedgwood (2007) points out the epistemic asymmetry between my own (religious) experiences and evidence, both of which guide me directly, and those of others, which can only guide me indirectly. This asymmetry explains why a vivid religious experience can have strong evidential force for me, but not for the person I tell my religious experience to. Indeed, there is an impressive collection of religious experiences in James (1902), and more recently in the Alister Hardy Religious Experience Research Centre, which has collected more than 6,000 reports since 1969. These experiences have a specific phenomenology, for example, "The experience was unbelievably beautiful, and I will never forget the quality of that bright white light. It was awesome." But their evidential force is hard to convey to third parties.

Note that conciliationists do not always change their views. For one thing, conciliationists have not given up their belief that conciliationism is right in spite of encountering many epistemologists who disagree with them. Under some circumstances it is reasonable to stick to your original beliefs, for instance, when it is more likely that the other party has made a mistake. But if you do not have any independent reason to think that your interlocutor, with whom you disagree, has made a mistake, conciliationism does require significant belief revision. Epistemologists have proposed several principles that would separate these two ways of responding to disagreement. One of these is the independence principle:

---

[3] See Christensen (2011) for an in-depth explanation of this terminology.
[4] An agent's credence in a proposition that p measures her degree of confidence in p.

> ***Independence:*** In evaluating the epistemic credentials of another's expressed belief about p, in order to determine how (or whether) to modify my own belief about p, I should do so in a way that doesn't rely on the reasoning behind my initial belief about p. (Christensen, 2011, 2)[5]

This principle can help reasoners guard against blatant circular reasoning ("Well, of course, since atheism is true, Linda must be wrong") and encourages epistemic humility. It maps out plausible courses of action in many cases of peer disagreement, such as Christensen's (2007) classic mental math case. In *mental math*, two restaurant goers split the bill and end up with different calculations of how much each owes, after adding the tip. It seems commendable to lower your credence in your original belief, say, that you each owe 23 dollars, in the face of the other person who has come up with a different amount, say, 26 dollars. However, sometimes a disagreement does not constitute evidence against one's own belief, but against the view that the other person is one's epistemic peer. Jennifer Lackey (2010) imagines the following situation, termed *elementary math*: I find out that my friend Harry thinks that $2 + 2 = 5$. This should not lead me to revise my belief that $2 + 2 = 4$ but rather lower my opinion of Harry's arithmetical capacities. Clayton could, in a similar vein, conclude that Linda is woefully misled about the question of God's existence, even if she is in general an excellent philosopher. Examples like these indicate that our intuitions about what to do in the face of disagreement will diverge depending on what the disagreement is about. And as we will see, the causes of the disagreement are also relevant.

This Element will examine different forms of religious disagreement (or agreement), and what we can learn from them. It is written in a broadly conciliationist spirit: I am working from the assumption that religious disagreement does provide higher-order evidence to one's religious beliefs, and that it should impact one's beliefs. In the next sections, I will look at disagreement with possible selves, with former selves, the epistemic significance of agreement about religion, the problem of religious expert disagreement and conclude by outlining the significance of philosophy of religion in religious disagreement. In each of these scenarios, I will show how conciliationism provides the right response, and how – at the same time – it does not mean we should necessarily become agnostic about all religious matters. The reason we should not be agnostic is that our own cognitive background constrains and colors the way we evaluate evidence. This allows us to maintain religious beliefs in many

---

[5] We will look at another proposed key principle that separates conciliationism and steadfastness, namely uniqueness, in Section 2.

cases, while nevertheless taking the religious beliefs of other people seriously, and often also revising our beliefs in the light of them.

Section 2 examines what it means to be in disagreement with possible selves: what if you had been born and raised in Afghanistan, where 99 percent of the population is Muslim, or in Papua New Guinea, where 99 percent is Christian? In all likelihood, you would have ended up holding the majority belief. Should this worry you? I will argue that it should not, but that the role of irrelevant influences still poses a problem at the macro level, specifically in constraining the range of viable hypotheses in the philosophy of religion. Section 3 looks at disagreement with your former self: if you converted to a different religious affiliation, can you be confident that your present belief is more likely to be right? I will argue that because religious conversion is epistemically and personally transformative, you cannot assume that this is the case. The best way to evaluate the beliefs of a convert (including yourself) is to engage in reasoned debate. Augustine's arguments in *De utilitate credendi* (*On the usefulness of belief*) will illustrate this approach. Section 4 looks at the flipside of disagreement, namely, the epistemic significance of agreement, in particular agreement about the existence of the supernatural. I will examine the argument from common consent, its merits and problems. Section 5 will analyze how we ought to respond to disagreement among religious experts. It looks at models of expertise and the proper response to expert disagreement. I propose a new model of expertise, the expert-as-teacher, incorporating advice offered by Maimonides in his *Guide of the Perplexed*. Section 6 concludes by showing that philosophical reflection can play a constructive role in religious debate.

I will now consider three arguments against conciliationism in the face of religious disagreement. The first is that religious disagreement is too messy and complex to be of philosophical interest. The second is that religious beliefs are insensitive to evidence and, therefore, cannot be revised in the light of higher-order evidence, rendering the discussion moot. The third is that relevant evidence in religious disagreement, such as religious experience, is private and cannot be shared between parties.

1.3 Is Religious Disagreement Philosophically Intractable?

Clear-cut cases like mental math elicit conciliatory intuitions: if I have no reason to think that I am better at mental arithmetic, it would seem prudent to be less confident when my epistemic peer and I come up with different numbers. But what about religion, politics, and all those other messy cases where we frequently find ourselves in disagreement? Maybe the concept of epistemic peer is not useful in such cases, as Adam Elga (2007) and others have argued. Suppose the belief we are interested in is the existence of God, as conceptualized in the Abrahamic traditions. Belief in this being is so tied up with our other beliefs, including political and moral beliefs, that it is hard to assess to what extent the other person is an epistemic peer. Kelli Potter (2013) has argued that in many cases it is difficult to gauge whether a religious disagreement is genuinely a disagreement.

Given the messiness of religious disagreement, one can see why the philosophy of disagreement – in spite of a clear and continued interest in the topic – tends to use clear-cut examples such as restaurant bills and simple visual perception, instead of real-world religious cases. However, excluding messy cases from epistemological consideration would leave us none the wiser about the rational status of beliefs we genuinely care about, such as in politics, philosophy, religion, and morality. We cannot use toy examples to reason our way into the more complex cases, in part because these toy examples already elicit differing intuitions (compare mental math with elementary math).

Arguably, the most interesting cases of disagreement occur when parties come with different sets of background beliefs. In some of these cases, the parties concerned consider their interlocutors to be peers, even though they do not know if the other person has exactly the same evidence or is equally virtuous. Can people in such cases still be called epistemic peers? It depends on one's notion of epistemic peerhood. The term "epistemic peer" was originally coined by Gary Gutting (1982), who described epistemic peers in terms of intellectual virtues. Aisha and Benjamin are epistemic peers if they are similar in attentiveness, thoroughness, and other virtues. Although this is the oldest definition of epistemic peerhood, and it is not often used in the recent literature, my survey on religious disagreement among academic philosophers (De Cruz, 2017) reveals that it is still popular. Sixty percent of surveyed philosophers favored a definition of epistemic peers as similar in intellectual virtues. Subsequent definitions focused on cognitive equality (Lackey, 2010), where Aisha and Benjamin are epistemic peers if they are similar in their cognitive capacities and limitations, and on evidential equality (Christensen, 2007), where they are epistemic peers if they have access to the same evidence for the domain under consideration. Sameness of evidence is a difficult criterion to meet. Even people who are closely matched in training and expertise, such as dissenting philosophers of religion, will not have access to the same evidence (e.g., they will have read different papers, gone to different graduate schools). Even peers who have access to the same evidence may not have assessed it correctly: perhaps they disagree fundamentally on which theoretical virtues to use in their discussion, such as simplicity, fruitfulness, generality, and coherence with background knowledge (Douven, 2010). Different weightings of such virtues could lead to divergent appreciations of natural theological arguments, such as the cosmological argument.

Suppose that we do not know whether parties have the same evidence, are cognitive equals, or are equally virtuous; does this make their disagreement epistemically irrelevant? This does not seem to be the case. Even if one's interlocutor is an epistemic inferior, such as an undergraduate student versus a professor, the disagreement does constitute some (albeit weak) evidence. There are, of course, many cases where we do not need to heed our epistemic inferiors (e.g., if my five-year-old and I come up with different numbers in a mental math problem, I do not need to revise my confidence that my calculation is right). But in many situations, we simply do not know if a person is in as good an epistemic position as we are (King, 2012). This is not just in messy religious disagreements but also even in more clear-cut cases such as mental math: Aisha may believe that she and Benjamin are equally good at mental arithmetic, but in reality Benjamin is significantly weaker.

Lackey (2010) favors the concept of *ordinary disagreement*. In a case of ordinary disagreement, Aisha and Benjamin consider themselves to be epistemic peers on the topic prior to their disagreement, and they come to realize that they disagree. In such situations, while we do not know whether the two parties are evidentially or cognitively equal, the mere fact of disagreement constitutes (defeasible) evidence. At the very least, the disagreement should lead us to inquire further into the other's position, by looking at the reasons he or she might have for holding it. For the purposes of this Element, I will understand epistemic peer disagreement as *ordinary disagreement*, unless otherwise specified.

1.4 Is Religious Disagreement Insensitive to Evidence?

A second worry for the philosophical discussion of peer disagreement is that religious beliefs might not be sensitive to evidence in the same way as ordinary beliefs are. When we argue about religion, it is not uncommon to hear appeals to personal satisfaction and meaning. When religious believers try to win converts, they will say things such as "Having a relationship with Jesus brings me joy!" rather than "Here are some reasons why I think the existence of God is more likely than God's nonexistence." Neil Van Leeuwen (2014) has argued that religious credences are largely insensitive to evidence. To Van Leeuwen, the belief "God is watching me" is cognitively distinct from the belief "The police are watching me." The latter belief would be vulnerable to evidence; the former would not. Religious beliefs are vulnerable to special authority, by people who are respected in their religious community and who fulfill a special role there. Although this claim that religious credences are insensitive to evidence is a descriptive one, not a normative one, it has repercussions for the epistemology of religious disagreement. How could we use religious disagreement as higher-order evidence if it were genuinely the case that our religious beliefs were psychologically invulnerable to evidence?

There is substantial evidence that religious beliefs are processed in a peculiar way. For example, Larissa Heiphetz and colleagues (2013) examined how adults and children reason about beliefs (both their own and those of other agents). They found that young children (aged five and older) already draw a distinction between fact-based beliefs (e.g., the size of germs) and opinion-based beliefs (e.g., which color is the prettiest). When asked whether two agents who disagreed about an opinion (e.g., whether broccoli tastes good) could both be right, children and adults tended to think that both agents could be right. For factual beliefs, they thought only one agent could be right. Religious beliefs fell somewhere in between, with adults responding at chance level about whether both agents could be right. Andrew Shtulman (2013) found that undergraduates are more likely to refer to authorities when justifying their belief in the existence of religious entities (e.g., angels, God, souls), compared to their belief in the existence of scientific entities (e.g., fluoride, electrons, genes).

However, religious beliefs are not unique in this way. Politically polarized beliefs such as beliefs about climate change and evolutionary theory in the United States show the same pattern of resistance to evidence, a pattern that might be explained by processing fluency (Levy, 2017). Although religious beliefs are intimately tied to factors such as personal identity and meaning, they still are to an important extent about factual matters (the same holds for political beliefs). This is why attempts such as Gould's (2001) non-overlapping magisteria, which aims to neatly separate the domain of science as the domain of statements of fact and the domain of religion as the domain of ought statements, fail. It is in practice often not possible to separate the factual claims from normative or preference ones in religious statements. If religion did not make any statement of fact but made only claims about value and ethics, these claims could not be justified using purported facts. For example, one could not argue that one should love one's neighbor because it pleases the Creator, because that is a (purported) statement of fact (God is pleased by neighborly love) (Worrall, 2004).

1.5 Private Evidence and Religious Disagreement

Peter van Inwagen (1996) has argued for the steadfast view by appealing to private evidence. We frequently have some (incommunicable) insight or experience that we might suppose the other person lacks. This can act as a symmetry breaker: when we have good reasons to think we have insight the other party lacks, there is no reason to move our beliefs in their direction. In a case that has become something of a classic in the epistemology of disagreement, van Inwagen expresses his puzzlement that David Lewis, a philosopher he admires, disagrees fundamentally with him about whether free will and determinism are compatible – van Inwagen thinks they are not; Lewis thought they are. To break the symmetry, he argues that he has some sort of special insight that Lewis, for all his perspicacity, lacks:

> But how can I take these positions? I don't know. That is itself a philosophical question, and I have no firm opinion about its correct answer. I suppose my best guess is that I enjoy some sort of philosophical insight . . . that, for all his merits, is somehow denied to Lewis. And this would have to be an insight that is incommunicable – at least I don't know how to communicate it – or I have done all I can to communicate it to Lewis, and he has understood perfectly everything I have said, and he has not come to share my conclusions. But maybe my best guess is wrong. (van Inwagen, 1996, 138)

This example demonstrates how adopting the steadfast view can erode the notion of epistemic peer: if van Inwagen believes his alleged epistemic peer to lack some insight he possesses, he does not really consider him a peer (at least not about the question of free will), but sees himself as in a superior position. What are we to make of such private evidence? In the religious domain, the obvious candidate for incommunicable, unshareable private evidence is religious experience. But atheists may also have nonpropositional, non-inferential evidence for their position. The occurrence of evils such as the suffering of innocent children may give the atheist an experience of God's nonexistence (Gellman, 1992).

Religious experiences are common, but less common than religious beliefs. A survey among ordinary believers by the Pew Forum indicates that 59 percent of Americans regularly have religious experiences,[6] which make them less common than the number of Americans who believe in God (around 90 percent in the same survey), or than people who consider themselves members of a religious denomination (more than 70 percent). Anthropological research by Tanya Luhrmann among evangelical Christians of the Vineyard communities in Palo Alto and Chicago indicates that religious experiences are dependent on

---

[6] www.pewforum.org/2015/11/03/chapter-2-religious-practices-and-experiences/

practice. Evangelicals learn to distinguish their own thoughts from those of God who speaks to them. This is, as Luhrmann (2012b, 39) puts it, "a skill they must master." They master it, gradually, using a variety of techniques such as individual and collective prayer, and more imaginative exercises such as imagining having a date night with God. This gives rise to a peculiar problem, which Luhrmann dubs an "epistemological double register" that she frequently encountered among the parishioners she studied (Luhrmann, 2012a, 380). In spite of the vivacity of their religious experiences, practitioners often remain unsure whether a particular religious experience is really of God or stems from their imagination. As one congregant put it prosaically, "sometimes when we think it's the spirit moving, it's just our burrito from lunch" (Luhrmann, 2006, 149). At the same time, they feel they are certain that God exists. This certainty is not a result of any given experience of God, which is highly ambiguous for them. The Roman Catholic mystic Teresa of Ávila (1577 [1921]) broached a similar problem. Religious experiences can be very vivid, but their memory and vividness quickly fade and leave people experiencing them unsure whether the experience was a figment of their imagination. (Teresa also discussed the possibility that they might be of diabolical origin – this would of course still bolster belief in a supernatural realm, but not necessarily in an all-good God.)

There are other problems with using religious experience as a symmetry breaker. The diversity of religious experiences precludes a straightforward interpretation along the following lines: Nobuyo is a Shintō priestess. She works in an urban Shintō shrine and regularly experiences the presence of *kami*, spirits who enter the shrine and are worshipped. She concludes from this that the spiritual phenomena of Shintō are genuine, and that *kami* exist. For this, she might use something like Swinburne's (2004) credulity principle: if it seems epistemically that *kami* are present, then probably *kami* are present. Other people have religious experiences that provide purported evidence of other religious claims, not easily compatible with Shintō (such as Abrahamic monotheism). Given that even religious experience is not a firm symmetry breaker, the standing of incommunicable insights is also doubtful. In any case, it works both ways: Lewis may have incommunicable insights about free will that are somehow denied to van Inwagen. If you have no special reasons to believe that you are less likely to be wrong, and the other seems an epistemic peer in other relevant respects, private evidence cannot break the symmetry, and so it cannot justify the steadfast position. In sum, it may be difficult in practice to know whether the people we find ourselves in religious disagreement with are peers. But even if they are not peers, their beliefs constitute some form of higher-order evidence for us.

2 Irrelevant Influences and Religious Disagreement

2.1 You Only Believe That Because . . .

The medieval theologian Abū Ḥāmid Muḥammad ibn Muḥammad al-Ghazālī (ca. 1058–1111) considered the role of irrelevant influences on religious beliefs. Al-Ghazālī was born in the Persian town of Tabaran, in the district of Tus (northwestern Iran), where he received a traditional Islamic education. As a young man, he moved to Nishapur, where he studied under al-Juwaynī, a prominent Ash'arite teacher. Ash'arism was an orthodox Sunni theological school that was mindful of scripture without being litera-list. It opposed the Mu'tazila, another philosophical theological school that prized reason as a source of knowledge and was heavily influenced by ancient Greek – particularly Aristotelian – philosophy.

Al-Ghazālī was very critical of Muslim philosophers who drew upon the ancient Greeks, collectively termed *falāsifa* (the philosophers); his main beef was with Ibn Sīnā (Avicenna) and his arguments directly challenged Ibn Sīnā's claims. In particular, al-Ghazālī was skeptical of philosophers' self-professed reliance on reason and argument. He argued that the philosophers were guilty of *taqlīd*,[7] uncritically accepting the views of Aristotle and other ancient philosophers. Like Christians and Jews, the philosophers had the misfortune of being "born into an un-Islamic atmosphere [*ghayr dīn al-Islām*], and their ancestors had pursued no better ways" (al-Ghazālī, 11th century [1963], 1–2). Orthodox Muslims, by contrast, received divine revela-tion that was properly transmitted to them through the Qur'ān and ḥadīth (Griffel, 2017). So, al-Ghazālī reckoned he had the correct religious beliefs, compared to Christians, Jews, and adherents to ancient philosophy. In his spiritual autobiography *Deliverance from Error,* he expressed more doubts about having the right religious views. He observed that children of Jews, Christians, or Zoroastrians tend to almost exclusively follow their parents' religion:

> [A]s I drew near the age of adolescence the bonds of mere authority (*taqlīd*) ceased to hold me and inherited beliefs lost their grip upon me, for I saw that Christian youths always grew up to be Christians, Jewish youths to be Jews and Muslim youths to be Muslims. I heard, too, the Tradition related of the Prophet of God [*ḥadīth*] according to which he said: "Everyone who is born is born with a sound nature [*fiṭrah*]; it is his parents who make him a Jew or a Christian or a Magian [Zoroastrian]." (al-Ghazālī, ca. 1100 [1952], 21)

---

[7] *Taqlīd* denotes the uncritical acceptance of testimony or authority of one person by another; it usually has a negative connotation.

This consideration of religious diversity was the start of a skeptical meditation, not unlike Descartes's *Meditations*. If religious beliefs, which are such a large part of one's views, are the result of the accident of one's birth, how can we know anything? Al-Ghazālī resolved to put his religious faith on firmer epistemological grounds. He considered, and rejected, sense perception as the prime source of knowledge, as it is sometimes wrong: it was generally known in al-Ghazālī's time that although the Sun appears to be smaller than a coin, it is larger than the Earth. Even our intellectual beliefs can be wrong, as we often hold mistaken and unfounded beliefs when we are dreaming. And given that our present earthly life is often compared to a dreamlike state when compared to what we will know in the afterlife, how can we know that our intellectual beliefs are right? In brief, al-Ghazālī cannot be confident that he successfully cast off the influences of his upbringing. How could he know that his attacks against the philosophers were justified, given that his own beliefs, like theirs, were heavily influenced by circumstances beyond his control? (We will consider his own responses to this question in Section 2.4.)

This worry is a familiar one: you only believe the tenets of a given religion or ideology because you were raised as a Muslim, a Christian, or an atheist. Irrelevant influences raise a skeptical challenge that is intimately tied to the epistemology of disagreement. Given that my religious beliefs are to a large extent a result of the accident of where and when I was born, how can I be justified in holding them, especially once I become aware of religious diversity? This question will be the focus of this section. The epistemological debate about such irrelevant influences focuses on uniqueness and permissivism. Uniqueness holds that for a given proposition p, "there is just one rationally permissible doxastic attitude one can take, given a particular body of evidence" (White, 2014, 312). Permissivism, by contrast, allows for some leeway: there is more than one rationally permissible doxastic attitude we can take given the evidence (Schoenfield, 2014). In this section, I will examine what irrelevant influences are in the shaping and maintaining of religious beliefs, and whether they raise epistemological worries for religious believers. I will argue that while we cannot escape these influences, we can let religious disagreement work to our epistemic advantage, both in philosophy of religion and among religious believers more generally.

2.2 How Irrelevant Influences Affect Religious Beliefs

When is an influence that shapes our beliefs irrelevant? Katia Vavova (2018, 136) proposes the following general definition of irrelevant influences:

An irrelevant influence (factor) for me with respect to my belief that p is one that (a) has influenced my belief that p and (b) does not bear on the truth of p.

Being raised in a particular religious community shapes one's religious beliefs to an important extent. People in relatively religious nations acquire more orthodox religious beliefs compared to people from more secular nations who are similar to them in other respects, such as gender, age, and education. This is in part because we learn religious beliefs from an early age on, but also because in predominantly religious nations, the pool of potential partners, friends, or co-workers contains more religious people. People have a tendency to adopt the beliefs of those around them; this conformist bias also plays a role in shaping religious beliefs. But even in more secular nations, we are not insulated from irrelevant influences. In such countries, the beliefs of parents play an important role in shaping their children's beliefs, whereas in more religious countries, parental influence on the religiosity of their offspring is weaker, and influence from the surrounding community is stronger (Kelley & De Graaf, 1997). These complex patterns indicate that where and when one is born have a large influence on the religious beliefs one has.

This is also true for philosophers of religion. In an open-question survey I conducted with 139 philosophers of religion (De Cruz, 2018), I found that nearly half of them (43.9 percent) mentioned religious upbringing or education as a reason for the beginning of their interest in philosophy of religion. Here is a representative answer to the question "Can you tell something about the factors that contributed to your specializing in philosophy of religion?" by a male associate professor at a small liberal arts college:

> I was raised Catholic and have a strong respect for that tradition. This respect has led me to be interested in other traditions as well. At the same time, as I have studied philosophy, I have been intrigued by arguments for atheism. My parents were deeply religious and intellectually engaged with their faith; this has surely had an influence on me.

Education, too, seems to have played an important role in the religious beliefs of many philosophers of religion who took part in this survey. In particular, introductory courses in philosophy have led, in some cases, to the loss of religious belief. Here is a response by a female full professor at a research-intensive university:

> When I was a child I was a very committed believer and participant in Christianity. I gradually lost my faith, and the finishing element was a section on philosophy of religion when I took an introductory philosophy course in my first year at university. The shock was huge and (believe it or not), I was somewhat suicidal: I felt I no longer had any meaning in my life.

I think, ever since then, I have been trying to understand what happened to me, and wondering whether I really needed to abandon my faith.

If she had gone to a different university, presumably one with a more religion-friendly introductory philosophy course, perhaps she might not have lost her faith. This echoes a worry by Jerry Cohen (2000) that the place you decide to study at would have a large influence on your subsequent philosophical beliefs. Cohen chose to study at Oxford, rather than Harvard, for his graduate degree. At the time, graduate students at Oxford tended to accept the analytic/synthetic distinction, whereas those at Harvard tended to reject it. This was no coincidence, and not the result of purely independent reasoning on the part of these graduate students, but the result of what they were taught:

I believe, rather, that in each case students were especially impressed by the reasons respectively for and against believing in the distinction, because in each case the reasons came with all the added persuasiveness of personal presentation, personal relationship, and so forth. So, in some sense of "because," and in some sense of "Oxford," I think I can say that I believe in the analytic/synthetic distinction because I studied at Oxford. And that is disturbing. For the fact that I studied at Oxford is no reason for thinking that the distinction is sound. (Cohen, 2000, 18)

Similarly, in some sense of "because," and in some sense of "Muslim education and upbringing," al-Ghazālī was predisposed to think the philosophers' arguments were incoherent. In his *Incoherence of the Philosophers*, he rejected twenty of their arguments, for example, that they cannot demonstrate that the world is pre-eternal (i.e., had an origin outside of time). The *falāsifa* believed that the world, like God, was pre-eternal, because it would be impossible for an eternal being to generate something temporal. Al-Ghazālī argued against this claim: God is not a cause, like other causes, and we can imagine that the world was created at a given time. If we can imagine that, it is possible, and an omnipotent being could have accomplished this (Griffel, 2017). Al-Ghazālī's arguments are sophisticated – he used philosophical tools such as possible worlds (what he called "alternative worlds") and modal logic, which were derived from Greek philosophy. But if he had been raised in what he called an "un-Islamic atmosphere" and had not been familiar with Ash'arism, he would likely, at the very least, have been friendlier toward those same arguments he so ardently opposed. This seems, on the face of it, troubling for philosophers of religion, and for adherents to religious beliefs (including atheists) in general.

What gives irrelevant influences their sting? Identifying this has been a subject of continued debate, especially on the question of evolutionary and cultural factors in shaping our moral beliefs. In what follows, I will outline two ways to spell out the worry: irrelevant influences make our beliefs unsafe (the safety objection) and irrelevant influences make our beliefs subject to an unacceptable arbitrariness (the arbitrariness objection).

2.3 The Safety Objection

Perhaps we should be worried about irrelevant influences on our beliefs because they make our beliefs unsafe. If I had been born in another culture, or another time, I would have had different religious beliefs. John Stuart Mill formulated the worry as follows:

> And the world, to each individual, means the part of it with which he comes in contact; his party, his sect, his church, his class of society; ... and it never troubles him that mere accident has decided which of these numerous worlds is the object of his reliance, and that the same causes, which make him a Churchman in London, would have made him a Buddhist or a Confucian in Pekin. (Mill, 1859, 35)

Mill makes two related observations, namely that religious beliefs of different times and cultures contradict one another, and that beliefs that were generally held in past cultures, or that are believed by most people in different cultures, are widely seen as erroneous, even absurd, by people who are part of our contemporary culture. He formulates the pessimistic induction that beliefs widely held today will be rejected in the future. The only way I can think that I am holding true beliefs is to assume that I am lucky, because it is easy to conceive that I would have ended up with very different beliefs. Tomas Bogardus (2013, 384) spells out this safety objection as a premise-conclusion argument:

1. If you had been born and raised elsewhere, else when, and formed religious beliefs using the same method you actually used, then, by your own lights, you easily might have believed falsely.
2. Therefore, your religious beliefs were not formed safely.
3. Therefore, your religious beliefs don't count as genuine knowledge.

One problem with this argument is that safety is a controversial requirement for knowledge. Agents sometimes seem to possess knowledge, even though their acquisition of it was a result of irrelevant influences. Let's look at a real-world example, where knowledge is unsafe but still plausibly knowledge. Belief in evolutionary theory and in human-induced climate change is highly polarized in the United States. While scientists almost universally accept these beliefs, the general public is divided about them. The majority of conservatives disbelieve both, and the majority of liberals accept both. More scientifically literate conservatives are, if anything, even more likely to reject the scientific consensus. Levy (in press) argues that this polarization is due to the way people gauge testimony. Because we often cannot check the content of testimony, we need to rely on cues that signal whether the informant is telling the truth. These cues can be divided into two categories: competence (to guard against learning from people who make mistakes) and benevolence (to guard against learning from people who want to deceive us) (e.g., Lane, Wellman, & Gelman, 2013). Conservatives and liberals use the same heuristics, but because the antiscience sentiments in conservative milieus have been so rampant since the 1970s, conservatives, while accepting scientists as competent, perceive them as less benevolent than liberals do. Thus, liberals are epistemically luckier than conservatives about scientific matters. Because liberalism is science-friendly (at least in the United States, and at least about these two topics), its "chains of deference trace back to the relevant scientific experts, and therefore to properly constituted collective deliberation." Conservatives are not so lucky: their chains of deference "end in 'merchants of doubt' ... or maverick scientists" (Levy, in press). This sociological phenomenon makes American liberals' scientific beliefs unsafe: if they had been born in a conservative family or environment, they would likely not have ended up with the correct scientific beliefs, but their beliefs are plausibly still knowledge.

Looking at al-Ghazālī through a Millian lens, he argued that although Christians, Jews, and Muslims acquire their knowledge in the same way (through deference to testimony), only Muslims have access to proper, undistorted, divine revelation. If he had good reasons to believe that the others are less likely to be right, then it is not a problem that he was lucky to be born into the correct religious atmosphere. While al-Ghazālī was able to refute the views of the philosophers using their own methods and could thus discredit them, this does not automatically vindicate his own beliefs. In *Deliverance from Error*, he argued that mystical perception through Sufi practice was able to provide such vindication. But as we have seen in Section 1.5, and will explore further on in this section, the community into which the mystic is born also colors religious experience. If you have reasons to believe you are right, then the luck of being born in a community that holds the correct beliefs does not preclude knowledge.

2.4 The Arbitrariness Objection

Another objection against irrelevant influences is that they seem to make our beliefs arbitrary, in a way that reduces (or perhaps even eliminates) their justification. This is the arbitrariness objection against permissivism (Simpson, 2017). Arbitrariness poses a problem for both conciliationists and steadfasters. Here is the problem for conciliationists: according to permissivism, there can be leeway in how we respond to evidence as long as we are using good epistemic standards (Schoenfield, 2014). But if that is the case, why should I revise my religious beliefs when I meet someone who holds a different set of beliefs? As long as we are both using good epistemic standards, there is no pressure to revise. Yet, conciliationists hold that beliefs of epistemic peers constitute higher-order evidence in the light of which we should reevaluate our beliefs. Thus it would seem that you cannot be both a conciliationist and a permissivist.

But steadfasters also face a problem if they wish to endorse permissivism. To see how, imagine that it is true that there are many rational ways to respond to the evidence for whether or not God exists. The total evidence relevant for God's existence (E) contains, for example, the apparent fine-tuning of cosmological constants in a way that is life permitting, and human-induced and natural suffering. Suppose that Anjelica says, "I think there are many rational ways to respond to E, but as far as I'm concerned, the evidence supports Anselmian monotheism, and I hold this belief with a credence of .7." How can Anjelica rationally endorse her own belief as well as allowing that other beliefs are rational, for example, Miguel's, who is an atheist, and only holds a .1 credence in the existence of any god?[8]

Roger White (2014) likens cases where irrelevant influences play a large role in our beliefs with having to ingest a belief-toggling pill that randomly causes one to believe not-p where one believed p before (or swapping the credence that p of .7 with one of .1). Believing that p with a credence of .7 is thus purely accidental; I might have believed otherwise. Is it rational to hold fast to this belief? The only way in which it might be is to assume that I've been lucky in ingesting the right pill or growing up in the right community (White, 2014), and that assumption seems unwarranted. This motivates uniqueness: there is only one way to respond rationally to a body of evidence. The arbitrariness objection thus raises a challenge to any kind of religious belief. It would seem that suspension of belief is the rational response in the face of religious diversity, as we cannot know we were lucky in holding the right beliefs. Even a motivated agnosticism cannot be maintained, because this position would also presumably be the result of irrelevant influences. This is not a desirable epistemic situation.

---

[8] The question of whether permissivists can also be conciliationists is a topic of continued interest and discussion (see e.g., Ballantyne & Coffman, 2012).

One way for the permissivist to respond is to argue that religious beliefs are not analogous to pill-popping cases. The pill-popping example presents an isolated belief, whereas religious beliefs are closely interwoven with other beliefs and are the result of many different irrelevant influences (rather than just a single factor), for example, family, education, friends, books one happens to read. The belief that God exists is often related to many other beliefs, such as attitudes to abortion, gay rights, and political orientation. Thus, where and when you are born is not like ingesting a pill that can leave you with a right or mistaken belief. It is something that shapes your whole attitude to the world, including how you respond to evidence.

The permissivist could also respond that we have different background conditions that make it rational for us both to respond to the evidence in different ways and to see the other person's beliefs as evidence. Several authors have argued along these lines. For example, according to Robert Simpson (2017) one could be a permissivist about a given question if the following conditions apply to my dissenting epistemic peer and me:

1. Our different views are due to our having different cognitive abilities and applying different epistemic standards.
2. The use of our epistemic standards is optimally truth-conducive for us, given the cognitive abilities that we have to work with in the application of our respective epistemic standards.

By cognitive abilities, Simpson (2017) means the abilities that we put into practice when applying epistemic standards. By epistemic standards, he means methods agents use to assess the evidence they have gathered. For example, two detectives give dissenting assessments of the evidence of a crime in a court of law. One detective is very good at gauging whether testimony is insincere (a human lie detector); the other is not as good in this, but she is excellent at holistically assessing the total evidence at the scene of a crime. It does not seem unreasonable for the former to place more weight on testimony, and for the latter to place more weight on the total evidence. Such constraints are still quite stringent, but they would allow for permissivist attitudes toward religious and other beliefs. Because our background environment has such a large influence on the religious beliefs we hold, we will end up with different cognitive abilities and different epistemic standards with respect to religious beliefs. Take two religious experts who disagree about the nature of God. One has been trained in religious practices from an early age, especially practices to cultivate awe and wonder, as in Judaism (Wettstein, 2012), and accords much weight to experiential evidence. His colleague is a biblical scholar who has a deep understanding of scriptural texts, but she is not trained in such practices.

It does not seem unreasonable for her to accord more weight to the evidence of written sources than to the occasional experiential evidence of God's existence that she has. The best we can do is work from these epistemic standards and use these tools to come to well-grounded, justified beliefs.

Can a response along these lines work for al-Ghazālī? His views were profoundly shaped by his own upbringing and education, but the philosophical tools he acquired while studying under al-Juwaynī did allow him to formulate novel objections against Muslim philosophers who rather uncritically accepted Aristotelian arguments for the eternity of the universe and other claims. It should also be noted that while al-Ghazālī's work is strongly influenced by Ash'arism, he does differ from this school in subtle respects (Frank, 1994). Take his notion of *taqlīd*, and its subtle differences with how the Ash'arites dealt with it. Like Ash'arite authors, al-Ghazālī saw a tension between uncritical acceptance of the testimony people hold in esteem (*taqlīd*) and religious knowledge. The Ash'arites believed that testimony, by itself, could not lead to knowledge. They considered intuition, perception, inference (inductive reasoning), and formal reasoning (deductive reasoning) as sources of knowledge. By contrast, according to al-Ghazālī, *taqlīd* could lead one to hold the right beliefs. In his *Incoherence of the Philosophers*, he argued that accepting testimony from proper sources, such as the prophets (as recorded in the *Qur'ān* and *ḥadīth*) could lead to knowledge, but that knowledge obtained through critical reflection is superior (Griffel, 2005).

The charge against the *falāsifa* can thus be refined: al-Ghazālī saw their uncritical acceptance of ancient Greek philosophy as a problem, because they prized their own reasoning, cleverness, and wit. However, if they were to give up their *taqlīd*, they would come to realize that these transmitted beliefs are wrong and would come to the true views of orthodox Islam. Thus, a complex picture emerges where al-Ghazālī sees it as incumbent upon people who are able to critically reflect to evaluate their beliefs and see whether they hold up to scrutiny. If we apply this to philosophers of religion or to any religious believers, it is inevitable that they are shaped by the religious traditions of their birth, but that does not prevent them from reflecting upon their beliefs. They should do this, especially if an interlocutor (perhaps coming from a different religious tradition) offers them reason to doubt their views. Indeed, it would be hubristic and intellectually dishonest not to do so. But if, on reflection, their original beliefs hold up, their justification increases.

The peculiar result of this approach is that it works regardless of the circumstances in which you were brought up. The total body of evidence for any religious position (e.g., the existence of God) is fiendishly complex and large. Most people will only have a partial grasp of E. But if they do the best they can, they can have justified religious beliefs regardless of the perspective they come from. In this picture, a philosopher or an ordinary believer who critically and honestly examines arguments for the existence of God can obtain a high degree of justification, as can contemplatives who seek out and cultivate their mind and habits to gain meaningful religious experiences, as Teresa of Ávila and al-Ghazālī recommended.

2.5 Making Religious Diversity Work in Philosophy of Religion

One may ask whether the strategy al-Ghazālī recommended for reflective thinkers works. Belief polarization is a well-attested collective phenomenon whereby people tend to diverge, rather than converge, in the face of disagreement. Several biases cause this phenomenon, including confirmation bias, which leads one to evaluate more positively evidence in line with beliefs one already holds. Even highly educated reflective thinkers are unaware of their own biases. For example, people consistently think that they are less susceptible to biases than the average American, their classmates in a seminar, or their fellow travelers (Pronin, Lin, & Ross, 2002). Given the bias blind spot, there is no way that al-Ghazālī (ca. 1100 [1952], 21) can confidently state that "the bonds of mere authority [*taqlīd*] ceased to hold me and inherited beliefs lost their grip upon me," because it is hard to know how biased one's own reasoning is. Moreover, in *Deliverance*, al-Ghazālī became more pessimistic about reasoning as a source of religious knowledge and argued that mystical experience (through practicing Sufism) would provide knowledge. However, mystical experience tends to vary with the religious traditions in which it occurs, so it is not clear that knowledge based on this would escape the arbitrariness objection. It is no coincidence that al-Ghazālī had mystical experiences that support Islam, while Teresa of Ávila had experiences that were in line with Roman Catholicism.

If individual debiasing is difficult and only has modest success, one way to address the problem of irrelevant influences is to let religious disagreement work productively. We can do this by actively encouraging or cultivating religious diversity, especially in a reflective forum such as philosophy of religion. This strategy has been proposed by philosophers of science such as Kitcher (1990) and Longino (1991). These authors have different motivations for why encouraging diversity of opinion and disagreement may be practically rational. Their recognition of scientific practice as a collective endeavor forms a common element. Philip Kitcher (1990) sees a mismatch between what is rational for an individual scientist to believe compared to what is rational for scientists as a group to pursue. Sometimes it is conducive to scientific progress that individual scientists hold unpopular or maverick views, even if these are not as well supported by the evidence as the mainstream view; for example, plate tectonics was a minority view in geology for more than half a century until it was vindicated by geomagnetism, biogeography, and other observations in the 1950s and 1960s. Agents who are driven by motives that are not purely truth oriented do better than agents who are only interested in the truth. The optimal epistemic situation is often one where agents combine a search for truth with less pure motives, such as a quest for fame, or trying to obtain a result quickly. Applied to the philosophy of religion, some authors have worried that philosophers of religion have an agenda; that is, they have less pure motives. They want to proselytize and are perhaps more biased than philosophers in other disciplines (Draper & Nichols, 2013). But this is not a problem in Kitcher's approach: it is fine if philosophers of religion have an agenda, as long as they are not all driven by the same motives.

Helen Longino (1991) has argued that even if scientists try to remain unbiased, they will still exhibit the biases of their research program, education, gender, race, and class. Contextual values, which are not directed at the truth, will inevitably play a role. One way to solve this problem is through standpoint epistemology – a powerless subject can have privileged knowledge because of her social situation (e.g., she can see hurdles or solutions invisible to others). But this will not suffice to eliminate biases. Hence Longino recommends the active cultivation of diverse points of view, a sharing of intellectual authority, which ultimately – through productive dialogue – facilitates transformative criticism. Applied to philosophy of religion, this would mean the active cultivation of viewpoints that are not mainstream. Given the preponderance of Christianity in the discipline, it could benefit from the cultivation of Muslim, Jewish, Mormon, Wiccan, Shintō, and other points of view. Moreover, given that the field of philosophy of religion is still overwhelmingly male and white, the participation of marginalized voices such as women, genderqueer individuals, and nonwhites would not only allow for the sharing of intellectual authority but also for insights on topics such as the atonement, free will, or the nature of God that will be colored by intersectional characteristics.

We can now see how irrelevant influences can play both a productive and a negative role in the philosophy of religion. We cannot overcome our biases that are a result of a lifetime of socialization and experiences – even if we try our very best, as al-Ghazālī and Descartes did. But with the particular cognitive mind-sets we have, we can do our best to arrive at true beliefs. This allows for a permissivist picture of religious disagreement. At present, academic philosophy of religion is predominantly white, male, and Christian. This poses constraints on the ideas that can be generated, leading to the problem of unconceived alternatives (posed by Kyle Stanford [2006] as a problem for scientific realism). Stanford observes that scientific communities have repeatedly failed to come up with reasonable alternatives to dominant scientific theories, although erstwhile unconceived alternatives are later confirmed by evidence and adopted by scientific communities. The same can be argued for philosophy of religion, which leaves large swathes of conceptual space unexplored.

Even if we assume that at least some of today's religious traditions capture meaningful parts of religious reality, thoughtful dialogue would be to our advantage. Take John Hick's (1988) argument for religious pluralism: the world is religiously ambiguous, it does not clearly favor one religious worldview over another, and it can be interpreted religiously or nonreligiously. Hick sees particular religious concepts such as Allāh, Viṣṇu, or the triune God as phenomenal interpretations of a noumenal religious reality. He uses the parable of the blind men and the elephant, where each blind person feels a different part of the elephant (e.g., the smooth tusks, the flexible trunk, the sturdy legs) and judge what they are feeling. Given that our understanding of the religious domain is shaped to a large extent by irrelevant influences, we will have a particular religious outlook. But this does not mean that the opinions of others hold no weight. If we accept that the religious domain is indeed complex and ambiguous – without perhaps going as far as to endorse Hick's Kantian distinction between noumenal and phenomenal – we can learn something from the religious beliefs of others. While the accident of where and when we are born poses serious constraints on our own religious beliefs, we can learn from the viewpoints of those who are differently situated. Jerome Gellman (1997) suggests a different way of looking at this. Apparently contradictory experiences of God point to an inexhaustible plenitude on God's part; for example, God is both personal and impersonal – hence he, she, they, it are experienced by some as personal (e.g., theistic religions) and by others as impersonal (e.g., Daoism).

To conclude, while the accident of where and when we are born leads to the arbitrariness objection, this does not necessarily mean we have to give up any articulate position on religious matters. As a matter of fact, we can use religious diversity to our epistemic advantage given that intellectual diversity helps communities of truth seekers to obtain beliefs that are more truthful and more justified. Given the complexity and ambiguity of the religious domain, such diverse perspectives shed different lights on the question of God's existence and related matters.

3 Conversion and Disagreement with Former Selves

3.1 Religious Conversion and the Independence Principle

Miguel and Catherine are both atheist philosophers and longtime friends from graduate school.[9] Miguel respects Catherine and believes she is his epistemic peer. Both of them have been raised in a liberal environment where atheism is quite widespread. But they have also carefully thought about theism. Neither of them is a philosopher of religion, but they know the arguments for and against theism, and they both agree that the arguments against outweigh the arguments for. As a result, both are quite complacent atheists: they think there is no serious case to be made for theism.

Miguel meets Catherine at a philosophy conference – it's been about a year since they last met. He has been looking forward to seeing his old friend. As they catch up over a cup of coffee, it becomes clear that Catherine is now a theist.

"But why?" Miguel asks, "Didn't you think all that theist philosophy is dubious motivated reasoning?"

"I changed my mind," Catherine replies.

This situation appears to be a case of peer disagreement. Miguel and Catherine are (presumably) equally thoughtful in the domain in question, and they have access to the same evidence. While their epistemic situation is not identical, they will still be similar enough to take each other to be epistemic peers, a situation that occurs frequently in everyday life. As we have seen in Section 1, epistemologists have debated whether one should conciliate, that is, revise one's opinion that p when faced with a disagreeing peer who holds that not-p or whether one can remain steadfast.

One principle that has been proposed to separate these two types of responses is the independence principle. Recall, this principle says that in evaluating the epistemic credentials of someone else's belief about p, I should not rely on my reasoning behind my initial belief about p when determining whether and how to revise my own belief about p. There are counterexamples to the independence principle, where one has a high justified belief that p, and where it does seem that one can rely on one's original reasoning. If someone truly believed that $2 + 2 = 5$, this would demonstrate that this person is, in all likelihood, not as clear-headed as you.

Would a religious conversion be more analogous to *mental math* or more like *elementary math*? Many people have a response along these lines: "I don't

---

[9] This section is adapted from "Religious conversion, transformative experience, and disagreement," *Philosophia Christi* (2018, 20[1]: 265–274). More information about *Philosophia Christi* can be found at http://www.epsociety.org/.

know what happened to Josh. He was such a reasonable guy, but then he joined Scientology. I think he's gone off the cliff," or, "I used to respect Amy, but now she is no longer an Evangelical Christian, I cannot respect her anymore." In such cases, people treat the conversion as a situation where one's epistemic peer has acquired such an outlandish set of beliefs that they begin to doubt the peerhood, akin to *elementary math*. In other cases, where the new belief is at least a live option (in the Jamesian sense), the case may appear more like mental math (e.g., "I'm not Jewish, but it does look like an interesting religion with a rich theology; Amy might be right for all I know, or I might be right"). There is a further problem for treating conversion cases as peer disagreements: religious conversions tend to be transformative. This makes it hard to assess whether the person is still one's epistemic peer, or what the proper response should be. As a result of this transformation, the beliefs of a dissenting peer, arising from a religious conversion, do not have straightforward evidential value.

3.2 Conversion as a Transformative Experience

Some experiences transform us, both in who we are and what we know. L. A. Paul (2014) has termed such experiences "transformative experiences." They are personally transformative, in that they change who you are as a person, and they are epistemically transformative, in that they give you new information by virtue of a particular experience that can only be obtained by having that experience. Paul has argued that we cannot rationally make decisions that will transform us because there is an asymmetry between who we are now and what we know now, and who we will be then and what we will know then. We cannot make a comparison between before and after to calculate the expected utility; for example, adopting a child may be a wonderful experience for my friend, but I may come to regret it. Yet, we often make life-changing decisions: choosing a subject of study, getting married, or joining a religious tradition. Not all transformative experiences are the result of conscious decisions. Enduring a long-term illness or becoming disabled is a situation few people choose, yet it transforms what they know (e.g., what it is like to live in the face of imminent death) and who they are (e.g., someone who became blind). The transformative nature of disability is illustrated by how disabled and non-disabled people think about their quality of life: sighted people tend to think being blind is a lot worse than blind people think it is, including blind people who were previously sighted (Carel, Kidd, & Pettigrew, 2016).

Is religious conversion transformative? Saul/Paul's conversion to Christianity on the road to Damascus suggests that a single transformative event can lie at the basis of conversion. As recorded in Acts 9 (in a third-person narrative) and the Pauline epistles such as Galatians 1 (in a first-person narrative), Saul of Tarsus was a Jew who persecuted the early Christian community. On his way to Damascus, where he was extending his mission to have Christians imprisoned, he had a dramatic religious experience: he saw a blinding light and heard the voice of the risen Christ, who asked him why he was persecuting him. Saul then got baptized and started missionary work for the nascent Christian church. This account of conversion in terms of a single dramatic experience shaped subsequent discussions of what conversion is like, for instance, in the work of early psychologists such as James (1902). Subsequent research into religious conversions suggests a more gradual pattern. Conversions are not single experiences, but rather the cumulative effect of many smaller experiences and decisions. Even among people who self-identify as born-again Christians, the majority experience a gradual, rather than a sudden, conversion to Evangelical Protestantism (Dixon, Lowery, & Jones, 1992). Nevertheless, religious conversions transform a person's system of beliefs (thus are epistemically transformative) and change their personality. This is not so much a change in personality traits, as it is in goals, feelings, attitudes, and life meaning (Paloutzian, Richardson, & Rambo, 1999).

Given that a person, post-conversion, is both epistemically and personally transformed, it becomes difficult to gauge whether a former epistemic peer is still so. For example, Jonathan Edwards has an extensive record of the deepening of his faith in several phases:

> [M]y sense of divine things gradually increased, and became more and more lively, and had more of that inward sweetness. The appearance of everything was altered: there seemed to be, as it were, a calm, sweet cast, or appearance of divine glory, in almost everything. God's excellency, his wisdom, his purity and love, seemed to appear in everything; in the sun, moon, and stars, in the clouds and blue sky, in the grass, flowers, trees, in the water and all nature; which used greatly to fix my mind. (Edwards, 1821, xxv)

How can we know that Edwards, post-conversion, is in an epistemically better position than before? How can Edwards himself know that this is the case?

3.3 Disagreement with One's Former Self

Conversion thus gives rise to two forms of disagreement – disagreement with one's former self and disagreement with friends and family. Let's look at someone like Catherine, who is now in disagreement with her former self. She now believes things she would have found implausible just a year ago. Should she accord more credence to her new beliefs? If conversion were solely the result of a careful, rational deliberation, it would seem proper that the convert is more confident about her beliefs post-conversion. However, conversion occurs as a result of several factors. These include the desire to be of the same religious tradition as one's family and friends and the desire for self-improvement and for having a religion that is more in line with one's self-image. For example, in a qualitative study of French young adults who converted to Islam (Lakhdar, Vinsonneau, Apter, & Mullet, 2007), several participants mentioned that they believed regular prayer and observing food taboos and Ramadan would help them to be more personally disciplined. Such concerns may be practically rational, but they do not say much about the truth or falsity of the beliefs they adopted.

The influential Lofland–Stark model of religious conversion (Lofland & Stark, 1965) outlines two basic conditions that prompt religious conversion: first, people must feel an acute need or tension within their religious problem-solving perspective, and second, they form affective bonds with members of the new religion/affiliation they convert to, which facilitates the step to the new religion/affiliation. This model has attracted much attention in the social study of religion. More recent sociological accounts of conversion (e.g., Kox, Meeus, & Hart, 1991) identify two types of attraction of religious movements to new converts: ideological, through offering a new perspective on life, and social, by providing a satisfactory social network.

Thus, conversion seems to be to a large extent the result of irrelevant causal factors, such as the presence of social groups that one might feel at home with and seek closer affiliation with. However, one's original religious beliefs (or lack thereof) are also largely the result of irrelevant influences. As we have seen in the previous section, there is a continued debate on whether irrelevant influences can act as defeaters to our beliefs. This debate often centers on the question of whether our response to the evidence allows for some latitude, as permissivists propose, or whether a total body of evidence only allows for one rational attitude, as proponents of uniqueness hold.

If we assume that sociologists are right and that most conversions are caused by a mixture of social and personal factors, few of which are relevant to the truth of the beliefs, how should one evaluate one's past self's beliefs? Vavova (2018) recommends that to evaluate the epistemic significance of irrelevant influences, we look at what causes these influences. If the influences give "good independent reason to think that you are mistaken with respect to p, you must revise your confidence in p accordingly – insofar as you can" (Vavova, 2018, 145). For instance, if a belief is the result of brainwashing or wishful thinking, this does seem to present substantial higher-order evidence that undermines the belief. Extreme cases of conversion that involve indoctrination or coercive force would thus be cast in a negative light, as indoctrination and coercion are in general poor belief-forming mechanisms. But for many other cases, which involve the typical mixture of social factors and personal motivations, it is not so clear whether these irrelevant influences provide the convert with good independent reasons that she is mistaken with respect to her new beliefs. The factors underlying conversion cases do not seem to be more epistemically vicious or benign than factors underlying original religious belief formation (e.g., parental religious affiliation).

A religious convert has one piece of higher-order evidence that someone who does not convert does not possess, namely first-person experience of changing one's religious beliefs in a deep and significant way: the convert knows that her religious beliefs can be changed.[10] This might lead converts to become more accepting and open to the religious views of others – after all, they had different religious beliefs prior to their conversion. If Catherine now holds beliefs she found implausible just a year ago, this tells her something meaningful not just about her current religious beliefs but also about the fragility and revisability of religious beliefs in general. Thus it would seem rational for a convert to remain open to the views of dissenting epistemic peers. By contrast, Miguel does not have the relevant experiences that presumably were at least in part the basis of Catherine's conversion. Given that he has not, he should remain open to the possibility that Catherine has relevant evidence that he lacks. Thus, conciliationism seems a rational response in the light of the conversion of a former epistemic peer. I will look in more detail at this question in the next section.

3.4 Disagreement with a Recently Converted Epistemic Peer

I will now look at the question of what (if any) epistemic conclusions Miguel can draw from Catherine's conversion, in the absence of further information (let's assume Catherine had to dash to the airport, so Miguel never gets to hear her reasons). Should it lower his confidence in his complacent atheism? One could argue that Catherine's conversion does not provide him with any new information. Miguel is presumably aware of the distribution of opinions about theism. He knows that most of the world population (about 85–90 percent) are theists, and most of them are monotheists (Zuckerman, 2007) and that a substantial number of academics (albeit less than 50 percent) are atheists (Gross & Simmons, 2009). He might also know that 73 percent of academic

---

[10] This is in addition to any first-order evidence that prompted the conversion, e.g., Paul's religious experience on the road to Damascus. Note that not all conversion cases involve such first-order evidence; some may be purely the result of social factors and do not offer any first-order evidence, but then the convert still has the second-order evidence of having converted.

philosophers are atheists (Bourget & Chalmers, 2014).[11] Since Miguel shares most of his background beliefs with academic philosophers, he would probably consider them as epistemic peers. Miguel could maintain his credences accordingly. At first blush, there does not seem to be any special information gained by an old friend having converted to a belief he does not share.

However, Miguel has acquired a new piece of information: someone with whom he had many background beliefs in common, and whom he has always respected as his epistemic peer, changed her mind on the question of theism. If he considers Catherine to be similar to him in many respects (e.g., shared graduate school experience, philosophers they both admire), they are similar in relevant background knowledge. Thus it would seem epistemically prudent for Miguel to at least follow up with Catherine (e.g., a simple email saying something like, "I have to confess I was a bit surprised that you're a theist now. Could you tell me more about it?"). After all, she may have reasons that he has not properly considered.

There is another reason why the conversion of a friend who was (at least previously) an epistemic peer is significant: we tend to attach more weight to the testimony of those who are close to us than to the testimony of strangers. Maybe this is because we can gauge the epistemic credentials of familiar individuals better. But familiarity alone does not explain the extra weight we accord to those near and dear to us. After all, if that were the case we would put more stock in people who are former friends, or in frenemies, and this does not seem to be the case (indeed, we tend to be more cautious when it comes to both categories). Being friends engenders epistemic partiality (Stroud, 2006). Toddlers already show a tendency to value the testimony of people close to them more than the testimony of strangers (Harris & Corriveau, 2011). This heuristic makes sense in the context of epistemic vigilance: since we not only need to sort out accurate from inaccurate testifiers but also those who are truthful from those who are deceitful, it makes sense to trust people who are well disposed toward us. Thus people have a tendency to place selective trust in those they see as benevolent: people with whom we have a mutually trusting relationship are less likely to deceive us (Sperber et al., 2010).

Trust in friends may also be valuable beyond purely epistemic reasons, just like self-trust is intrinsically valuable (Pasnau, 2015). Intellectual theorizing should not be seen as purely dissociated from our emotional lives: sometimes it makes sense to have our beliefs accord with those of our friends. This indeed often happens in the case of conversion, where people convert to the religious tradition of friends or relatives. For such reasons, Miguel should be more

---

[11] But see De Cruz (2017), where 50.2 percent of surveyed philosophers were atheists.

diligent in following up Catherine's reasons for converting. And perhaps like-wise, Catherine should be diligent in following up with Miguel to explain her reasons for converting. I will now look at a case study of conversion that illustrates why reasoned debate is the proper response to a friend's, and one's own, conversion.

3.5 Rational Argument and Conversion

The African theologian Augustine of Hippo (354–430) converted from Manichaeism to Christianity. In both religious traditions, he was an apologist, a teacher, and an evangelist. His letter *De Utilitate Credendi* (*On the Usefulness of Belief*) is addressed to Honoratus, a student friend. Augustine converted his friend to Manichaeism with much difficulty and in this letter set himself the unenviable task to try to convince his friend to convert to Christianity. But why should Honoratus, whom he previously persuaded of the merits of Manichaeism, now trust Augustine?

> For Augustine to achieve his purposes, Honoratus would have to be persuaded of Augustine's trustworthiness while discounting Augustine's much earlier evangelistic campaigns as a Manichee. Honoratus would also have to grant that Augustine himself had not been deceived a second time as he appears to have been misled the first time when he was persuaded by the Manichees. (Asiedu, 2001, 128)

The letter is revealing in that Augustine does not dwell on his own conver-sion experience, as he does elsewhere, for example, in his *Confessions* (4th century CE [1961]), as a source of knowledge. Rather, the letter focuses on biblical hermeneutics (the discrepancies between the Old and New Testaments, which Manicheans often pointed out as reasons to reject Christianity) and on high-level epistemic principles such as trust and credulity. The letter examines the reasons Manicheans gave for rejecting Catholic doctrines and argues that these reasons were mistaken. In this way, Augustine argues that Honoratus's (and his former self's) reasons for accepting the Manichaean doctrine were mistaken:

> Well, they harangued at great length and with great vigor against the errors of simple people, which I have since learned is extremely easy for anyone to do who is moderately educated; and if they taught us any of their own doctrines we thought we must maintain it because nothing else occurred to us to set our minds at rest. (Augustine, 5th century [1953], i, 2, 292)

The passage in viii, 20 recounts Augustine's own faith journey (what born-again Christians would call their "testimony"). He first reveals that he was already "in a state of serious doubt" about Manichaeism when he last parted from his friend, and that his doubt grew even more after he saw the under-whelming performance by the famous Manichean Faustus: "You remember, his coming to explain all our difficulties was held out to us as a gift from heaven. Well, I recognized that he was no better than the others of the sect, except for a certain eloquence he had" (Augustine, 5th century [1953], viii, 20, 306). The account of his own conversion anticipates the later fuller testimony in *Confessions*, especially Books 5 and 6. While Augustine does not use his own conversion as a source of evidence to Honoratus, he nevertheless presents it as a model that Honoratus can emulate. For example, he draws close parallels between his own former doubts (now happily resolved), and Honoratus's present doubts. This echoes the conciliationist position in the epistemology of disagreement. Recall, the conciliationist position holds that beliefs of others we respect as our peers provide significant evidence (in part because our peers may have reasons or arguments we may not have considered properly) and call for belief revision.

The letter (particularly sections vii–xi) also develops an intricate philosophy of testimony, where Augustine asserts that all knowledge must begin in trust of those who have proper authority, rather than in reason. He gives the example of the trust we place in our parents:

> How will children serve their parents and love them with mutual dutifulness if they do not believe that they are their parents. That cannot be known by reason. Who the father is, is believed on the authority of the mother, and as to the mother, midwives, nurses, slaves have to be believed, for the mother can deceive, being herself deceived by having her son stolen and another put in his place. (Augustine, 5th century [1953], xii, 26, 313)

To Augustine, the chief problem with Manicheans is that they do not recognize the importance of trust in testimony of those who have proper epistemic authority. Instead they hold up a mirage of how we should acquire beliefs: "they promise to give to those whom they attract a reason even for their most obscure doctrines" (ix, 21). Thus, they are not being intellectually honest with their adherents and converts, because it is simply not possible to give reasons for obscure doctrines, without resorting to trust in authoritative testifiers.[12] I will return to the topic of epistemic authority in the next section.

In *De Utilitate Credendi* Augustine sees testimony merely as a basis of belief. In his *Confessions* he also regards it as a basis for knowledge (King & Ballantyne, 2009). Yet, in the former he clearly sees testimony as a precondition for knowledge, as many people would lack the relevant

---

[12] This holds also for those who study the sciences. At some point, one needs to trust those with authoritative knowledge, as it is impossible to experimentally verify everything for oneself.

reasoning skills to work out religious truths for themselves. Augustine draws an illuminating parallel between friendship and trust in testimony. Against those who do not think that testimony can be a useful source of belief, Augustine (5th century [1953], x, 23, 309) argues as follows: "I do not see how anyone who accepts that as true can ever have a friend. For if to believe anything is base, either it is base to believe a friend, or without such belief I cannot see how anyone can go on speaking about friendship." While it is not made explicit, it is clear that Augustine here is appealing to his friend to read his arguments with more charity and patience than he would read the arguments from a Catholic writer he does not know, with the charity one owes a friend. The tone through-out the letter underlines this point, with Augustine frequently expressing understanding at what must be a surprise to his friend, for example, "You are amazed, I am sure. For I cannot pretend that I was not formerly of a very different opinion" (vi, 13, 301); he frequently anticipates objections Honoratus might have, such as, "But you will probably ask to be given a plausible reason why, in being taught, you must begin with faith and not rather with reason" (ix, 22, 308).

Overall, *De Utilitate Credendi* shows a good model of peer disagreement in the face of conversion. Augustine's aims in the letter are modest. As he points out in his closing paragraphs, he does not refute the Manichean doctrines or defend Catholic ones. Rather, he aims to show that the arguments that Manicheans have offered against Catholic doctrines (namely, alleged discrepancies between the Old and New Testaments) are not as strong as he previously believed. He also argues that Manichaeism does not live up to its own standards of belief based on reason, rather than testimony – a standard that Augustine also demonstrates to be unattainable. Along the way, Augustine can also demonstrate to himself (as he did at length in his *Confessions*) that he is now in a better epistemic position than his pre-conversion self. Even though Augustine may not be justified in thinking he now holds the correct doctrines, his new beliefs are based on more sophisti-cated grounds, whereas his previous reasons for rejecting Catholic doctrines proved to be inadequate.

3.6 Thoughtful Disagreement

The case of religious conversion presents a series of difficulties for traditional accounts of epistemic peer disagreement, because conversion is a transforma-tive experience: it is difficult to decide whether a convert is in a better epistemic position post-conversion. Conversion is rarely the outcome of a rational decision process, but the result of irrelevant influences such as personal tension and the religious views of friends. This was almost certainly the case for Augustine, as we can see in passages throughout *De Utilitate Credendi*, for example,

> When I departed from you across the sea I was already in a state of serious doubt; what was I to hold; what was I to give up? Indeed my hesitation grew greater day by day from the time that I heard the famous Faustus. (Augustine, 5th century [1953], viii, 20, 306)

Most cases of conversion are not caused by forces that are more pernicious than the ones that gave rise to the original set of beliefs (e.g., beliefs of one's parents). Given that both self-trust and trust in friends are valuable for epistemic and non-epistemic reasons, it does not seem wrong to accord prima facie weight to a friend's new set of beliefs if one saw this friend as an epistemic peer prior to conversion. Rational argument, as illustrated by Augustine's *De Utilitate Credendi*, can play a crucial role in evaluating peer disagreement caused by conversion. It not only helps one's friends to critically evaluate their beliefs but also allows the convert to critically reflect on her own beliefs.

4 What (if Anything) Can We Infer from Common Consent?

4.1 What Common Consent Might Mean

Much work in social epistemology has focused on disagreement. There is comparably little work on the epistemic significance of *agreement*. In a variety of everyday situations, finding yourself in agreement that p will often justifiably increase your credence that p. If I work out a tricky mathematical equation and I find that my epistemic peer has the same result, I justifiably become more confident that I am right. I can become even more convinced I am right if a great many people (of various mathematical abilities) arrive at the same result, independent from me. The same intuitions are elicited by more complex cases, for example, if two medical doctors converge upon the same diagnosis, it would seem right for them to accord more confidence to it. This is especially the case if they came to their diagnoses independently (Goldman, 2001). But even if they did have a common source, for instance, they might endorse the diagnosis of another medical doctor who is highly respected in her field, agreement can have epistemic significance. (I will say more on the role of source-independence later on in this section.)

Agreement has some epistemic significance, but how much weight should we attach to it? As we saw in Section 2, philosophers from various traditions have expressed reservations about uncritically accepting the consent of the religious community to which one happens to belong. To al-Ghazālī, as to many other medieval Muslim philosophers, *taqlīd* (mindless trust in testimony) is inferior to reasoning. It may be acceptable for the layperson but not for philosophers. Mill agrees:

> [T]o a thinker the argument from other people's opinions has little weight. It is but second-hand evidence; and merely admonishes us to look out for and weigh the reasons on which this conviction of mankind or of wise men was founded. (Mill, 1874, 156)

However, until the seventeenth century, theologians regarded common consent as substantial evidence for the existence of God. The argument from common consent, also known as the *consensus gentium*, establishes the truth of theism through its near universality. Joshua Rollins (2015, 84) gives the following formulation of the argument:

P1: Belief in God is (nearly) universal.

P2: For any given proposition p, if belief in p is (nearly) universal, p must be true.

P3: So, if belief in God(s) is (nearly) universal, God(s) must exist.

∴ God must exist.

Stated baldly in this form, the argument is not very impressive. Examples of beliefs that had near universal consent and that turned out to be false are legion, including about comets bringing disease and misfortune, or about the intellectual capacities of women. Yet, *consensus gentium* was among the most popular natural theological arguments in the Early Modern period, with proponents such as John Calvin, Pierre Gassendi, and John Wilkins. But it fell out of favor in the eighteenth century, and today it is hardly mentioned in major anthologies and reviews of natural theological arguments. In part, it lost its appeal because of increasing doubts about the reliability of the cognitive mechanisms that were thought to be at the basis of theistic belief, as will be shown in the next section. But to some extent, it fell out of fashion because of an increasing epistemic individualism, exemplified by authors such as Descartes and Locke, who focused on the individual thinker and his appeal to reason and argument. As we saw in Section 1, this epistemic individualism was a consequence of an epistemic crisis – a loss of confidence in the medieval religious, moral, and scientific consensus. However, the social nature of belief formation has experienced something of a revival in social epistemology. Social epistemologists, like traditional epistemologists, focus on how agents form beliefs and acquire knowledge. But unlike traditional epistemologists, they see knowledge production and belief formation as a primarily social enterprise. Since social mechanisms play an important role in the acquisition of religious beliefs (as we saw in Section 3), questions about their reasonableness should take into account what others believe and how we deal with socially acquired knowledge.

It is useful to reevaluate the common consent argument in the light of social epistemology. This section will review three versions of the argument and gauge their strengths and weaknesses: an early and representative version by John Calvin, Linda Zagzebski's argument from self-trust, and Thomas Kelly's argument that common consent is evidence. I then propose a fourth version, making use of newly developed tools in social epistemology, which formalize the intuition that if you find yourself in agreement with others, you can (under suitable conditions) attach higher credence to your beliefs. One surprising result of applying these new tools is that diversity of religious opinion can strengthen the argument from common consent. But overall, I will argue, common consent only has weak evidential value.

4.2 The Original Argument from Common Consent: From Innateness to Truth

Most traditional versions of the argument from common consent proceeded in two inferential steps: from common consent to innateness, and from innateness to truth. The reason why belief in God is near universal is that God implanted the belief in our minds. In this way, God figures in the explanation for common consent. The following formulation by Calvin exemplifies this two-step process:

> There is within the human mind, and indeed by natural instinct, an awareness of divinity ... God himself has implanted in all men a certain understanding of his divine majesty ... [T]here is no nation so barbarous, no people so savage, that they have not a deep-seated conviction that there is a God ... From this we conclude that it is not a doctrine that must be first learned in school, but one of which each of us is master from his mother's womb and which nature itself permits no one to forget. (Calvin, 1559 [1960], Book 1, chapter 3, 43–46)

Calvin makes empirical claims about the prevalence of religious beliefs across cultures, which would receive scrutiny in the following centuries, as Westerners came increasingly into contact with people from other religious traditions due to exploration, colonialism, and trade. The awareness of divinity (*sensus divinitatis*) is a hypothesis that explains the widespread belief in God.

The *consensus gentium* lost its philosophical appeal in part because this two-step inference became increasingly problematic (Reid, 2015): it was unclear whether belief in God was really innate, especially, as Hume (1757) and others observed, given that there were many societies in which belief in God was absent. Religious belief may be widespread, but theism is not, and even religious sentiments are not cross-culturally universal. As Hume observed:

> The belief of invisible, intelligent power has been very generally diffused over the human race, in all places and in all ages; but it has neither perhaps been so universal as to admit of no exceptions, nor has it been, in any degree, uniform in the ideas which it has suggested. Some nations have been discovered, who entertained no sentiments of Religion, if travellers and historians may be credited; and no two nations, and scarce any two men, have ever agreed precisely in the same sentiments. It would appear, therefore, that this preconception springs not from an original instinct or primary impression of nature, such as gives rise to self-love, affection betwixt the sexes, love of progeny, gratitude, resentment; since every instinct of this kind has been found absolutely universal in all nations and ages, and has always a precise determinate object, which it inflexibly pursues. (Hume, 1757, Introduction, 1–2)

Moreover, even if we grant that religious beliefs are widespread, this does not show that theism is true, because the mechanisms that lie at the basis of religious belief formation might not be truth conducive. Hume (1757) argued that an inability to explain and control future events was at the basis of polytheism, which he considered to be the earliest form of religious belief. Humans anthropomorphized the environment, which gave them a sense of control – they could now cajole and beseech the gods. Since wishful thinking and fear are not good belief-forming mechanisms, common consent to God's existence was vulnerable to a rebutting defeater. A rebutting defeater to p gives us reason for believing not-p, whereas an undercutting defeater to p gives one reason to suppose that one's ground for believing p is not sufficiently indicative of the truth of p (Pollock, 1987). For example, if I have evidence that a friend could not have known that p, I have an undercutting defeater for her testimony. But if I have evidence that she was lying to me that p, I have a rebutting defeater for my belief that p, formed on the basis of her (false) testimony. If religious beliefs were the result of unreliable cognitive mechanisms, we would have fresh reasons to doubt the veracity of these beliefs. Hume's arguments against *consensus gentium* hinge on details of how religious beliefs are acquired and on their distribution across cultures. He did not have good firsthand evidence about the latter but used unreliable reports of travelers and historians.

A thorough assessment of the common consent argument would thus require an extensive review of the cross-cultural distribution of religious beliefs and their acquisition. This is beyond the scope of this Element. I will here focus on the *sensus divinitatis* claim and evidence from cognitive science that is relevant for it.

The discussion about theism and its cognitive origins has seen a revival in the past few decades. According to Alvin Plantinga (2000), belief in God can be properly basic, just like our belief in other minds, an external world, or the past. Classic foundationalism holds that beliefs can only be properly basic if they fall into one of the following categories: they are incorrigible, evident to the senses, or self-evident. Any belief we hold, to be justified, must either be properly basic or derive from beliefs that are properly basic. Plantinga argued that many beliefs that we hold without explicit reasoning, sensory evidence, or argument are properly basic. These include the belief that other minds exist, that the past exists, and that there is an external world. We cannot know for certain that other people have minds, as internal mental states are not evident to our senses, and they are not self-evident either (as is shown by the fact that most nonhuman animals, very young children, and people with autism lack the ability to attribute beliefs to others). Yet belief in other minds is properly basic. If God instilled in human beings a *sensus divinitatis*, and if it is properly functioning, in a congenial environment, the beliefs could be properly basic in the way Plantinga suggests.

Kelly Clark and Justin Barrett (2010) have argued that the cognitive science of religion provides support for the idea that there would be a *sensus divinitatis*. They distinguish between Calvin's version of the *sensus divinitatis*, which is an innate belief in God, and Plantinga's version, which conceptualizes the *sensus divinitatis* as dispositional: it is elicited by particular experiences, such as of awe-inspiring natural beauty or morally relevant situations. Clark and Barrett identify two components to the *sensus divinitatis*: theory of mind and agency detection, also known as the Hyperactive Agency Detection Device (HADD).

Theory of mind is our ability to explain the behavior of other agents by attributing desires, beliefs, and other mental states to them. Thanks to theory of mind, we are able to understand actions that otherwise would be puzzling, such as someone acting on the basis of a false belief or searching for an object that is no longer where it was originally placed. Four-year-old children already differentiate between the mental states of God and those of limited agents: they predict that God, but not their mother, would know the contents of a closed box (e.g., Barrett, Richert, & Driesenga, 2001). There is also tentative evidence linking theory of mind directly to religious belief: in one study (Norenzayan, Gervais, & Trzesniewski, 2012) being on the autistic spectrum predicted decreased belief in God, and mentalizing deficits – a reduced ability in theory of mind – mediated this relationship.

HADD is an alleged mechanism (or set of mental mechanisms) that allows us to distinguish agents in our environment. The anthropologist Stewart Guthrie (1993) proposed that humans are prone to detect agents in their environment because it makes evolutionary sense to do so, as the costs of false negatives (failing to detect an agent) far outstrip the costs of false positives (mistakenly detecting an agent). For example, hikers tend to mistake boulders for bears but not bears for boulders, because not spotting bears in time could have potentially dire consequences, while misinterpreting boulders just gives them a little jolt. Barrett (2004) and others have further developed this theory, arguing that agency detection is hyperactive, that is, prone to make false positives. These are a result of the expected payoffs of false negatives and false positives. Given the low cost of a false positive, and the high cost of a false negative, we can expect HADD to misfire frequently. This would give rise to religious beliefs, which are subject to further cultural development. For example, some movement seen in the forest is elaborated into a belief in forest spirits.

Clark & Barrett (2010) argue that *sensus divinitatis* consists of theory of mind and HADD, and they call this the "god-faculty." It has components both of Calvin's nativist account, which sees religious beliefs as diffuse and underdetermined, and of Plantinga's dispositional account, as religious beliefs can be elicited by particular experiences. One problem with this proposal is that HADD and theory of mind are not the only mental mechanisms that are involved in religious belief. For example, promiscuous teleology, the tendency of young children (and adults) to attribute purpose and design to the world around them, might contribute to the formation of religious belief (e.g., Kelemen, 2004). The tendency of humans, from infancy onward, to over-attribute causation and to prefer agents as causes could underlie arguments for the existence of God, such as the cosmological argument, along the following lines: the universe is caused, and an agent is a plausible cause of its existence (De Cruz & De Smedt, 2015). One could further expand the god-faculty until all relevant contributing cognitive faculties are subsumed under it.

A second more serious problem is that researchers have not found consistent evidence for a link between HADD, theory of mind, and religious belief. Several authors have attempted to find a causal relationship between the propensity to over-attribute agency and religious belief, but they have failed to do so (see Van Leeuwen & van Elk, in press, for an overview). The role of theory of mind in religious belief formation remains contentious too, for example, contrary to Norenzayan et al. (2012), Lindeman, Svedholm-Häkkinen, & Lipsanen (2015) found no correlation between theory of mind and religious belief, and only a modest correlation between teleology and religious belief. Even if HADD plays a role in religious belief formation (e.g., researchers may not have implemented the proper research design to test for this), it is unclear whether this would vindicate the idea of a *sensus divinitatis*. For HADD is supposed to misfire frequently, eliciting many false positives, in addition to detecting the agents who are really present. In the absence of enough information on how HADD operates and what role (if any) it plays in the formation of religious belief, any attempt to establish the presence of a *sensus divinitatis* based on HADD is premature.

It is possible that the failure to find clear causal relationships between cognitive mechanisms and religiosity indicates a lack of the right empirical measures. As it stands, current empirical evidence does not support Calvin's two-step *consensus gentium* from innate religious belief to the truth of theism (the second could not be established through science in any case, given its methodological naturalism). Even if there were strong evidence for such a causal path, Calvin's argument would be vulnerable to a problem of under-determination. Religious beliefs are cross-culturally diverse. Scholars in the cognitive science of religion do not think that monotheism is the default religious position. Rather, the proposed cognitive mechanisms that lie at the basis of religious belief would support a wide variety of religious beliefs. Calvin and Plantinga have a response to the problem of religious diversity: the noetic effects of sin. As a result of the Fall, human cognitive capacities are marred and ideas about God have become distorted. As De Cruz & De Smedt (2013) have argued, this solution presents its own problems: within the cognitive science of religion, there is no naturalistic parallel of the Fall to the naturalized *sensus divinitatis*.

This does not indicate that any common consent argument based on the innateness of religious beliefs is unsound. However, the lack of empirical support for a *sensus divinitatis* and the lack of a naturalistic account of the noetic effects of sin make it hard to naturalize the common consent argument. One could still argue that there is a *sensus divinitatis* and that God has implanted it to instill religious belief in people across cultures, not taking on board the cultural baggage of the Fall. This argument does not stand or fall with empirical evidence. But note that traditional defenders of the *consensus gentium*, such as Calvin, make use of empirical claims to bolster the view that God has implanted a sense of the divine in all people across cultures. In the light of this, I will now examine common consent arguments that look purely at the distribution of beliefs, while remaining agnostic about their genealogy.

4.3 Common Consent, Self-trust, and Evidence

Linda Zagzebski (2011) proposes a common consent argument that appeals to the notion of self-trust. According to Zagzebski, humans have a natural desire for truth, and they believe that this desire can be satisfied using their faculties and cognitive processes, including perception, memory, and reasoning. As a result of this, we have a basic, non-reflective and inescapable self-trust, a trust in our own cognitive faculties to obtain the truth. For example, I want to know what the weather is like (desire for truth); I look outside and see many clouds in the sky. I trust my faculties and believe that it is cloudy (self-trust). In addition, we also often try reflectively to get at the truth; Zagzebski terms this reflective quality "epistemic conscientiousness." It comes in degrees. Just a little of it is a natural extension of our pre-reflective self-trust. But some people try especially hard to get to the truth, using metacognitive skills to see if they are doing well (e.g., checking the result they obtained twice, and asking themselves questions such as "Have I overlooked evidence?" "Am I in an echo chamber?" "Can I use another method to check my results?"). While there are limits to self-reflection, Zagzebski believes that we can make a reasonable assessment of how epistemically conscientious we are.

Once we accord trust to ourselves, Zagzebski believes, we are obligated to accord the same trust to the faculties of others, because "[m]any other people appear to me to be just as conscientious as I am when I am as conscientious as I can be" (Zagzebski, 2011, 29). If a large number of people have a given belief, such as that Belgium became an independent country in 1830, we have some reason to believe that this is true, because people have a natural desire for truth and we should trust them because we have self-trust. Similarly, given that millions of people believe in the existence of God, I have reason to trust them. This trust is defeasible. For example, it might turn out that people who believe in God are not as conscientious in their beliefs as atheists or agnostics. But prima facie, the trust ought to be accorded. Elizabeth Fricker (2014) thinks this move is problematic, because it assumes that others are epistemically like us, which is an empirical matter and not something we can decide a priori. Moreover, trusting others is not unavoidable in the same way as trusting ourselves is, using the following analogy:

> Suppose the only way across a chasm, to escape a deadly predator, is over a rotten-looking bridge. So I have no choice but to rely on it to take my weight, taking a leap of epistemic faith in doing so. This in no way means

that I am guilty of culpable inconsistency, if (having survived my ordeal!)
I refuse to cross other similar, rotten-looking bridges, when I am not constrained by compelling practical motives to do so. (Fricker, 2014, 197)

Even if the cognitive dispositions that generate religious beliefs are similar for me and other people, it does not follow that I should extend my self-trust to others. What we would be observing is that many people are crossing the rotten bridge rather than awaiting their fate with the predator. This says something about their relative assessment of bridges and predators, perhaps that they have a better chance of survival crossing the bridge than staying in the vicinity of the deadly (presumably hungry) predator. Once we take this line of reasoning, *consensus gentium* is no longer based on self-trust, but on a form of evidence.

Thomas Kelly (2011) has formulated (in the same edited volume as Zagzebski) a *consensus gentium* argument that regards religious belief as a form of evidence. For Kelly (2011, 142), the underlying reasoning behind any argument from common consent is an argument to the best explanation: "I am justified in concluding that p is the case on the basis of the fact that p is the dominant opinion in the group only if the truth of p is part of the best explanation of the fact that p is the dominant opinion in the group." For religious belief, he considers the following datum.

Datum: A strong supermajority [i.e., more than 60 percent] of the world's population believes that God exists.

If the best explanation for the widespread belief in God is God's existence, then we can infer that God exists based on the datum. Kelly considers several objections. For example, the datum might be false because "God" does not have the same referent. But the strongest argument he finds is that the datum is insignificant because the supermajority was not produced by independent convergence. In many and indeed probably most cases of common consent, majority opinion is not produced independently. The fact that the majority of Belgians believe Belgium became an independent country in 1830 is due to their learning this at school. However, the truth of this fact is part of the explanation that Belgians (if they remember what they learned at school) generally believe it. The best explanation for why the school curricula include this is that Belgium indeed became an independent country in 1830, and thus in spite of a lack of independent convergence, common consent here satisfies Kelly's necessary condition of figuring in the best explanation.

Is this the case for belief in God? This is unclear. Let's take Kelly's (2011) example where there is no other evidence for a given belief. Suppose I see the bins standing outside of my neighbors' house on a day that the bin collection normally does not occur, I may reasonably conclude my neighbors believe the bin collection will happen today. The most plausible explanation for this is not that my neighbors have suddenly become delusional, but that they have information that, for some or other reason, is not available to me. It seems rational to me to put my bin out. If we look at common consent to belief in God, it is a result of a complex mix of cognitive and sociological factors. Although this mix is more complex than the causal origins of the belief in the bin collection day, one could argue that the existence of God is a reasonable explanation for why the belief is so widespread. But it is unclear whether an analogous argument could be made for God.

4.4 Synergy and the Epistemic Significance of Consent

Under some circumstances, peer agreement that p does not only heighten your credence that p but also raises the credence higher than either peer's initial credence. Take, for example, two detectives or two medical doctors who consider each other as epistemic peers and come to the same suspect or diagnosis. One has a credence of .95, and the other .97. Upon learning that my epistemic peer has reached .95, while I have .97, it seems plausible for me not to split the difference (lower my credence to .96) but become even more confident. Kenny Easwaran et al. (2016) formalize this intuition in their concept of "synergy." Synergy allows two agents to update their credences to a higher credence than their initial credences, using the Upco rule:

$$p(A_i)+ = \frac{p_i q_i r_i \cdots}{\sum_{j}^{k} = 1 p_j q_j r_j \cdots}$$

Here, we have peers P, Q, and R who have prior credences p, q, and r. Upon learning each other's credences about A, they should update their credences according to the Upco rule. For example, suppose Catherine has a .8 credence that God exists, and she encounters Anita, who has a .7 credence that God exists, and Catherine considers Anita her epistemic peer on this matter. If she were to split the difference, she would have to downgrade her credence to God's existence to .75. But with the Upco rule, Catherine can upgrade her credence up to .9, as follows:

$$\frac{.7 \times .8}{.7 \times .8 + (1 - .7)(1 - .8)}$$

Thus, if you encounter many epistemic peers who have a high credence that God exists, you can increase your credence. It becomes relevant to see how belief in God and credences in belief in God are distributed, and whom one's epistemic peers might be. If we take "God" to mean the God of the Abrahamic monotheisms, worldwide belief in God was at about 55 percent in 2010.[13] This falls short of common consent but is still very widespread. If the definition is more encompassing to also allow for monotheistic strands of Hinduism and other traditions, the belief goes up to about 70 percent. In 2014, about 89 percent of the US population believed in God (slightly down from the previous years) and about 63 percent believe in God with certainty, with a further 20 percent who are fairly certain that God exists.[14] "Certain" and "fairly certain" are not precise credences, but they are, we can assume, quite high, significantly more than .5. Thus, a religious believer who finds herself surrounded by religious believers can update her credence to a higher one.

However, religious belief is significantly lower among academics, and even more so among philosophers, as we saw in Section 3. Among a sample of philosophy faculty members, the percentage of atheists and agnostics in elite universities in the United States is about 60 percent (Ecklund & Scheitle, 2007), but if small liberal arts colleges, teaching-intensive state schools, and community colleges are included, the percentage of faculty members who believe in God or a higher power is about 75 percent (Gross & Simmons, 2009). Among a sample of philosophers (mainly drawn from elite universities in the United States, the UK, and Canada) 72.8 percent disbelieve in God (Bourget & Chalmers, 2014). But most philosophers do not consider religious questions in their academic work; only a small minority (philosophers of religion) do. The majority of philosophers of religion (more than 70 percent), unlike philosophers in general, lean toward theism (Bourget & Chalmers, 2014; De Cruz, 2017). From these numbers, it is difficult to say what the common consent would be that is relevant to a philosopher who considers the existence of God (probably, most readers of this Element are in this position).

Whether there is common consent among one's epistemic peers thus depends on the group one considers relevant for this question: the world population, the US population (assuming one lives in the United States; the percentage of theists is lower in other Western countries), academics, philosophers, or philosophers of religion. The notion of epistemic peerhood is restricted to domain, so an epistemic peer is in this case a peer about the

---

[13] www.pewforum.org/2012/12/18/global-religious-landscape-exec/.

[14] www.pewforum.org/religious-landscape-study/belief-in-god/.

question of God's existence. It is unclear whether academics or philosophers would be in a better epistemic position in respect to this question. Throughout this Element, I use the notion of ordinary peer disagreement (i.e., disagreement with people we consider to be our epistemic peers in day-to-day life), rather than using a particular notion of peerhood (e.g., evidential, cognitive). But even with this loose notion, it is hard to find a non-question-begging way of determining who might be our epistemic peers about God's existence. Different religious traditions employ different standards of what would count as relevant evidence and what would put one in a better epistemic position, including mystical experience, scripture, theological training, a properly working *sensus divinitatis*, or the right kind of faithful attitude. Given that people across the world are interested in the question of God's existence, and that it is not clear who would count as an epistemic peer, it seems prudent to use the global population as the relevant reference class.

Epistemologists take it that consensus that p strengthens one's justification for believing that p, and that disagreement that p, especially with an epistemic peer or superior, should decrease one's justification. However, there are several cases where diversity can increase our trust in the consent that remains. Take disagreement in the scientific domain. When scientific experts disagree, for example, about the precise mechanisms involved in natural selection, this is often taken as evidence that these theories are incorrect. But, as Dellsén (2018) has argued, dissent between scientists can indicate that their conclusions are not purely a result of sociological factors, such as scientists who unthinkingly follow popular opinion or one scientist's authority. Frequent dissent in fact bolsters our confidence in scientific ideas for which there is widespread consent, such as climate change and evolution through natural selection, even though scientists may differ in their opinion on how quickly climate is changing or how natural selection operates. Zach Barnett (in press) argues that when we evaluate the evidential value of common consent, we need to consider the expectation that the agents would reach the same conclusion. He takes the case of two students who reach the same answer on a logic exam, but it turns out that one student has uncritically copied the other. Here, it seems straightforward that agreement between these two students lends no extra weight to the solution being the correct one. However, suppose one student is copying the other, but she checks his results while doing so. She does not correct them because she thinks that he is right, and so they end up with the same result. In this second case, the agreement does lend more weight to the solution.

Barnett's rule can explain why common consent in echo chambers, such as Facebook reactions to news, is of very limited value. Suppose Saray, a liberal philosopher, is engaged with her friends on Facebook on whether ending net neutrality would be overall worse for most Internet users.[15] The topic of net neutrality is one with which few people have familiarity, and even experts cannot foresee the ramifications of ending it. Moreover, this is a politically charged topic: liberals tend to be pro net neutrality, whereas conservatives are more split about the issue. Saray believes that ending net neutrality is going to be bad and accords a high credence (.8) to this. But because she mainly interacts with other progressives, it is unsurprising that they too think it will be bad to end it. Suppose her friends Naomi and Benjamin also think ending net neutrality will be bad, with credences .7 and .9. Using Upco, they would arrive at an updated credence of .988. (Since the resulting credence of each agent is higher than his or her initial credences, this is an instance of synergy.) However, given that they are in an echo chamber with likeminded people, it is unsurprising that they will agree. Common consent only increases my credence if I should not expect, in advance, to reach the same conclusion as my peers. That would suggest Saray should not use Upco to update her belief in net neutrality. By contrast, if Saray's conservative friend Calum also says that scrapping net neutrality will be terrible, she should be more confident it will be bad, because he does not share her liberal viewpoints.

Applying this to religious beliefs, religious diversity can counter the view that religious beliefs are purely the result of following authority. Indeed, new religious movements such as the Church of Jesus Christ of the Latter Day Saints, which Joseph Smith founded following the religious diversity he saw in his community in New York, are evidence of independent reflection on the question of God's existence and other questions about ultimate reality. The fact that so many people across cultures hit upon similar religious beliefs (e.g., in superpowerful and super-knowing agents, with whom they can interact by performing rituals) is an intriguing convergence. The lack of an empirical basis for a *sensus divinitatis* makes it difficult to defend a Calvin-style common consent argument, which moves from common consent to innateness, and from innateness to truth. But it makes the more direct common consent argument more plausible. Insofar as religious beliefs across cultures have a common core of belief in supernatural agents, and we cannot expect in advance to see such consent, the belief has some prima facie evidential value.

---

[15] Net neutrality is the principle that Internet service providers must treat all data on the Internet the same.

5 Religious Expertise and Disagreement

5.1 The Importance of Religious Expertise in Disagreement

An extensive division of labor governs our everyday lives. We depend on experts, including engineers, plumbers, medical doctors, philosophers, mathematicians, physicists, priests, and car mechanics. We not only defer to experts, but we often outsource questions we have about various practical and theoretical problems to them. This divide between experts and people who depend on them is widening, given that expert knowledge is increasingly becoming specialized and extensive. As a result, it becomes increasingly harder for nonspecialists to evaluate the claims experts make. This lack of transparency becomes a problem when experts disagree. In the religious domain, experts disagree about fundamental questions such as whether God exists, whether God became incarnate, whether there is divine revelation, and how this is manifested. They also disagree about minutiae such as whether the Trinity should be understood through a social or Latin model, or whether there will be free will in the afterlife. (I will discuss in more detail further on in this section who might be a religious expert, but for the time being, you can think about such people as priests, theologians, philosophers of religion).

At first sight, a novice confronted with such disagreements has few resources to evaluate who is right and whom to trust. This gives rise to the following puzzle: how can laypeople know which expert is right, and which expert to trust, if they cannot evaluate the truth of what experts are saying? This is what Alvin Goldman (2001) termed the "novice/expert problem"; the problem of how a novice, while being a novice, can make justified judgments about the credibility of rivaling experts. Next to the practical problem of choosing to trust particular experts, expert disagreement in a domain D also gives rise to deeper epistemological worries about D, namely, whether the disagreement should lower our confidence in statements made by experts in D or even whether there are any experts in D. Religion is a field rife with expert disagreement, both within and especially across different denominations and faiths. The novice/expert problem is also important because disagreements can often be reduced to expert versions. Suppose you have an atheist (Abby) and a theist (Theo) who are not experts, debating the possibility of theism.

ABBY: I can't believe you buy into all that theist humbug. Seriously, if God existed he would prevent bad things from happening.

THEO: But God may have good reasons to let bad things happen. Perhaps, it serves some greater good.

ABBY: Okay, that sounds plausible sometimes. But why would he allow, say, my sister to die of cancer? And if she had to die, why did it take months and cause so much pain? Why did he allow my father to abuse me when I was a child?

THEO: Look, I don't pretend to know the answer to all of that, and I'm sorry about what happened to you and your sister. I don't want to minimize what you went through. But God's reasons may just be inscrutable to us.

Conversations like these take place in everyday contexts of religious disagreement and often are reminiscent of more sophisticated philosophical discussions. In this example, Abby's formulation of an evidential argument from evil reminds one of Rowe's (1979) classic example of a fawn that dies in a forest whose suffering does not seem to promote any greater good, and Theo ultimately appeals to skeptical theism.[16] This section focuses on the novice/expert problem of expert disagreement in philosophy of religion. My primary aim is to provide a model of expertise that can help solve the novice/expert problem. In the next subsection, I ask who might qualify as a religious expert, drawing on different theories of expertise outlined in the epistemological and cognitive science literature. I then look at two models of deference to experts, the expert-as-authority model (Zagzebski, 2012) and the expert-as-advisor model (Lackey, 2018). While I argue that the latter is a better model in the face of disagreement, I show that it does not provide a clear heuristic of what to do in the face of disagreement among experts. To remedy this, I forward a new model, the expert-as-teacher, which provides a useful set of heuristics that novices can use when dealing with expert disagreement. I examine the recommendations of the medieval theologian and philosopher Maimonides in *Guide of the Perplexed* (12th century [1963a]) on how to deal with conflicting opinions of Jewish religious experts as a way to flesh out this model.

5.2 Who Counts as a Religious Expert?

Across cultures, religious experts are common. In societies with little division of labor (beyond sexual division of labor), including small-scale hunter-gatherer and horticultural cultures, religious experts are among the few experts that a community can support. They are shamans, healers, and priests, called upon to help members of the community deal with a variety of practical and epistemic problems. Consider *baganga* (singular: *nganga*), religious experts in Central Africa who call upon ancestor spirits on behalf of their

---

[16] See also Levinstein (2015, Appendix B), who has outlined a formal model to show how disagreements between agents are isomorphic to their hypothetical expert versions.

clients (Janzen, 1978). To do this, the *nganga* creates special containers called *minkisi* (singular: *nkisi*) to summon and focus the power of ancestor spirits. The ancestors are called to help in a variety of situations such as curing illness or infertility, and to protect against misfortune. A *nganga* is a respected individual whose status and earning increase if he or she is perceived as effective. The making of *minkisi*, often in the shape of bowls and anthropomorphic figures, is a tricky practice that requires extensive knowledge of symbolism: figurines are covered with nutshells or seashells (metaphors for wombs), mirrors as symbols for the boundary between the ancestors and the living, teeth and nails to signify a spirit's forcefulness, and particular plants with various meanings. *Baganga* are considered experts in their communities because of both their extensive knowledge of the spirit world and their ability to summon spirits to help humans with problems they face in everyday life.

This example indicates that religious expertise is, at least in part, a social phenomenon. The practical element of *baganga* expertise is crucial: their reputation is to a large extent determined by the degree to which they can help clients by engaging in successful religious practice. Their theoretical knowledge, for instance, about which *minkisi* are most appropriate under specific circumstances (e.g., the use of nutshells and seashells in *minkisi* to combat infertility) is an integral part of this.

Philosophers and cognitive scientists have proposed different notions of expertise in the literature. I will briefly review them and then examine their suitability for thinking about religious experts. One influential notion of expertise is the *veritistic* notion, which sees an expert as someone possessing a large store of knowledge (at minimum, true beliefs arrived at in a justified way), compared to nonexperts. For example, Goldman conceptualizes an expert as follows:

> An expert (in the strong sense) in domain D is someone who possesses an extensive fund of knowledge (true belief) and a set of skills or methods for apt and successful deployment of this knowledge to new questions in the domain. (Goldman, 2001, 92)

For many domains of expertise, we do not know whether what the experts have is knowledge. This is not only the case for religion but also for other domains where we assume there are genuine experts, such as philosophy. Philosophers do not have independent measures to assess whether their intuitions in such domains as ethics and epistemology are the correct ones and need to rely on consensus in their community (Cummins, 1998). Given that consensus correlates with the strength of intuitions, but not with their correctness (Nagel, 2012), this makes it hard for philosophers to assess whether they have knowledge or true belief. The *evidential* notion of expertise faces a similar problem. According to this notion,

> S is an expert with respect to domain D if and only if S possesses substantially more and/or better evidence concerning propositions in D than most people in the relevant comparison class. (Goldman, 2018, 6)

Unfortunately, what counts as evidence is not clear-cut. For instance, in the religious domain there is disagreement about whether private religious experiences constitute more relevant evidence (this view is held in more experientially based, mystical traditions such as Sufism in Islam or Pentecostalism in Christianity), or whether an extensive knowledge of doctrine and scriptural texts would make one an expert. There seems to be no straightforward way to adjudicate what counts as evidence and what should have more evidential weight. The difficulties of establishing expertise in terms of knowledge or evidence have led some authors to focus more on the social role of expertise, and to cash it out in terms of skills and practice. For example, Collins and Evans argue that "contributory expertise enables those who have acquire [an expert skill] to contribute to the domain to which the expertise pertains: contributory experts have the ability to do things within the domain of expertise" (2008, 24). Being able to contribute to a field (not merely understand it and grasp the theoretical elements of it) indeed captures an essential element of expertise. But this definition still leaves out the social nature of expertise, and the ability to help others. Goldman's CAP definition of expertise attempts to incorporate this:

> S is an expert in domain D if and only if S has the capacity to help others (especially laypersons) solve a variety of problems in D or execute an assortment of tasks in D which the latter would not be able to solve or execute on their own. S can provide such help by imparting to the layperson (or other client) his/her distinctive knowledge or skills. (Goldman, 2018, 4)

These notions of expertise help us to define who might be an expert, but they do not identify experts among members of our community, nor do they offer clear guidelines for the extent to which we should defer to experts, especially if their testimony conflicts (the novice/expert problem mentioned earlier). I will look at two solutions to the novice/expert problem in the next subsection. Each provides concrete recommendations on what a novice should do when faced with an expert in D when she wants to learn something in D. The main difference between these approaches is that Zagzebski (2012) recommends suspending one's own judgment and Lackey (2018) does not.

5.3 Two Models to Solve the Novice/Expert Problem

Zagzebski (2012) puts forward a defense of epistemic authority, a topic that she acknowledges does not sit easily with the contemporary emphasis on individualism and free choice. Political philosophers have attempted to justify political authority, as it seems inescapable that we are subject to it. But what about epistemic authority? Although it seems less inevitable, we do find ourselves frequently in the situation where we have to rely on experts (e.g., making a diagnosis of illness, predicting how climate will change). Zagzebski argues that deference to epistemic authority can be rational. It does not require being able to believe on someone else's command, which is controversial (although, see Peels, 2015 for a recent defense that we can choose to believe). It merely requires preemption. Preemption is the process by which reasons for believing something a person might have are replaced by other reasons, in this case, reasons based on what an authority says or does. The preemption thesis, drawn from Joseph Raz, goes as follows:

> *Preemption*: The fact that the authority has a belief *p* is a reason for me to believe *p* that replaces my other reasons relevant to believing *p* and is not simply added to them. (Zagzebski, 2012, 107)

On the face of it, bracketing one's own reasons in favor of an epistemic authority (an expert) seems like a bad procedure to form beliefs. What reasons would we have for doing so? Zagzebski believes that there is a straightforward justification: suppose I am a novice in D, and E is an expert in D, and I am wondering about forming the D-relevant belief that p. Given that E knows more about D than I do, she is more likely to be right about p than I am if I were to try to figure out whether p is true on my own. To argue for preemption, Zagzebski forwards the track record argument. Suppose that you are in an experiment where a light flashes green 80 percent of the time, and red 20 percent of the time. You need to predict when the light flashes green to obtain a reward. Given that the change in color occurs at random, the rational and utility-maximizing strategy is to always predict a green light. Although rats and pigeons maximize, humans tend to perform suboptimally by only predicting green in 80 percent of cases, ending up with fewer correct guesses, about 68 percent.[17] Analogously, if E is more likely to get it right than I am as a novice, I do better if I trust her in all matters concerning D. That is why Zagzebski thinks that we should treat experts as authorities (expert-as-authority model).

While this argument might work if I know just one expert (or have reasons to think a person is an expert) in D, things become a bit trickier when there are

---

[17] Unfortunately, while many authors mention this experiment, I was unable to trace its source.

several experts in D, especially if they disagree. As Lackey (2018) cautions, if there are multiple experts who disagree fundamentally about a number of issues, you had better pick a good one. This caution seems especially warranted in the religious domain, where following the wrong religious expert potentially not only has detrimental epistemic effects (leading one to have wrong beliefs about the religious domain) but also potentially bad moral effects (leading one to hold morally unpalatable beliefs), or perhaps even ill salvific effects. The worry does not only arise in the case of disagreement but also in the ideal case Zagzebski has in mind where there is only one viable epistemic authority I can follow. If I have to replace any reasons for belief in D with those of E, what reasons would possibly lead me to consider E an expert in the first place? Maybe I should trust E because many others tell me that she is an expert. At some point, it becomes difficult and implausible to bracket away one's own reasons for belief even in a domain one is not an expert in. As Lackey (2018, 234) cautions, such deference "provides all of the resources for rendering rational the beliefs of paradigmatically irrational communities," including Young Earth creationists, Flat Earthers, or white supremacists.

Given the problems that the expert-as-authority model faces, Lackey recommends an alternative, the expert-as-advisor model. She starts out from several cases where we use expert advice and come to our own considered views as a result. Expert witnesses in a trial can provide members of the jury with compelling reasons for why p is true, but the jury will take these reasons into consideration together with other pieces of evidence to reach its verdict. Similarly, ethics consultants at hospitals can advise on whether a given procedure is in the best interest of the patient and other interested parties, but the decision to, say, refuse or follow a given treatment is up to the medical doctors, patients, and sometimes their families (as in the decision to turn off a ventilator that keeps a patient alive). In such cases, we do not have to replace our reasons with the beliefs of the expert. To generalize:

> An expert that is an advisor does not give authoritative testimony or preemptive reasons for belief; rather, her testimony provides evidence for believing a given proposition and, in this way, offers guidance. (Lackey, 2018, 238)

An expert opinion is regarded as a relevant piece of evidence, next to other pieces of evidence. Lackey (2018) motivates this solution to the novice/expert problem by appeal to the puzzle of isolated secondhand knowledge (first described in Lackey, 2011). This occurs when someone knows that p through expert testimony and lacks any other relevant information. It would seem that it is improper to assert that p in such cases, even though one knows that p (which would be a counterexample to the sufficiency condition of the knowledge norm of assertion, which says that knowing that p is a sufficient condition for asserting that p). One of the cases she uses to elicit the intuition that flat-out assertions of experts do not give sufficient reasons for accepting a given belief that p is DOCTOR:

> Matilda is an oncologist at a teaching hospital who has been diagnosing and treating various kinds of cancer for the past fifteen years. One of her patients, Derek, was recently referred to her office because he has been experiencing intense abdominal pain for a couple of weeks. Matilda requested an ultrasound and MRI, but the results of the tests arrived on her day off; consequently, all the relevant data were reviewed by Nancy, a competent medical student in oncology training at her hospital. Being able to confer for only a very brief period of time prior to Derek's appointment today, Nancy communicated to Matilda simply that her diagnosis is pancreatic cancer, without offering any of the details of the test results or the reasons underlying her conclusion. Shortly thereafter, Matilda had her appointment with Derek, where she truly asserts to him purely on the basis of Nancy's reliable testimony, "I am very sorry to tell you this, but you have pancreatic cancer." (Lackey, 2011, 34–35)

Note that in this scenario, Nancy is a student – neither an expert, nor a peer (Benton, 2016). If the case is modified whereby the person reviewing the evidence on behalf of the doctor is a fellow oncologist, or even a team of oncologists, or a student nearing completion of her training, the assertion seems less improper. Maybe the intuitions in the DOCTOR case also have to do with the fact that the doctor cannot *explain* to the patient why the evidence points to the pancreatic diagnosis. As Matthew Benton (2016, 506) argues, it is unclear whether "we expect that experts always have an obligation to explain to a non-expert what is behind the formation of their opinion." We do seem to expect of expert testimony, more than of ordinary testimony, that an expert can explain the reasons behind her testimony. Lackey (2018) argues that cases of secondhand isolated knowledge favor her expert-as-advisor model over Zagzebski's expert-as-authority model. Experts need to function as advisors to nonexperts; to do so, they need to be able to explain or back up their claims.

However, the puzzle of isolated secondhand knowledge does not exclusively favor the expert-as-advisor model. It is compatible with a number of other solutions to the novice/expert problem, such as the one I will outline in the next subsection, the expert-as-teacher. The expert-as-advisor model does not solve the novice/expert problem when we are faced with disagreeing experts.

The question of which expert a layperson ought to trust when experts disagree is now replaced with the question of which advisor a layperson should turn to, in case several advisors disagree. Moreover, while the advisor model provides more resources to dismiss the beliefs of irrational communities such as white supremacists and Young Earth Creationists as irrational, there is no clear mandate against following the advice of such communities.

To sum up, the expert-as-advisor model is not constrained enough in providing guidance for which expert to trust. It also fails to capture that sometimes we ought to treat an expert as an authority. In the advisor model, we are free to choose whether or not we should follow the ethics consultant, believe the expert witness, or heed the fitness coach. But if a medical doctor recommends an antibiotics treatment for sepsis, it would be ill advised to dismiss his counsel in favor of that of an herbal doctor. More generally, if listening to genuine experts becomes optional (as the expert-as-advisor model suggests), it would be acceptable for policy makers to ignore experts, for instance, on climate change. If experts predict that climate change will likely have devastating consequences, it would be prudent to heed them. A plausible model of expert testimony would need to satisfy at least the following two desiderata: on the one hand, it is not a good idea to bracket one's own reasons. On the other hand, experts do have genuine authority that requires some form of deference.

5.4 The Expert-as-Teacher

Conceptualizing experts-as-teachers provides an alternative to the previous models. As we have seen, the main shortcoming of the former model is that it asks laypeople to cordon off their own reasoning in favor of the expert's opinion. The latter model is not constrained enough: in some situations we really should treat an expert as an authority. The novice/expert situation is often a novice/teacher situation. Cross-culturally, teaching is one of the main ways in which expertise is transmitted. This does not always occur in the form of explicit, verbal instruction. It can also consist of a teacher directing the attention of the learner to a relevant part of the task at hand, or providing negative or positive feedback on a task the learner has performed (Legare, 2017), for example, a potter pointing out the correct speed with which the potter's wheel turns, and helping to adjust the apprentice's clay on it.

Ellen Fridland (in press) has argued that teaching is crucial for complex, cumulative culture (unique to humans) because it allows for innovation. Thanks to teaching, a learner knows what parts of a culturally transmitted skill are relevant, how they fit together, and how the skill might be improved.

By contrast, pure imitation is more conservative. Children tend to over-imitate, that is, to imitate features of a process that do not contribute to the successful outcome of that process (Nielsen, Mushin, Tomaselli, & Whiten, 2014). This observation is cross-culturally robust and has been replicated several times. Adults are not immune to it either, copying causally irrelevant actions when they imitate the solution to open a puzzle box (Whiten et al., 2016).

Why would we lose time and energy copying irrelevant elements of an action? Part of it may simply be caution. Many cultural skills are opaque, and it is often unclear to a novice which parts of the action matter. Suppose, for example, that a plant is only edible when it is extensively treated: it has to be dried, pounded, and boiled before consumption. Without a detailed toxicological analysis, we cannot know which parts of this process make the plant lose its toxicity. It is better to be safe than sorry and to copy all the actions, rather than hasten the process and risk being poisoned. Even among experts, over-imitation might occur for this reason. As Nick Shea (2009) notes, scientists will often follow the minutiae of a protocol, for example, a particular dose of solvent (10 ml instead of, say, 25 ml), because of the time and resources involved in carrying out the experiment. By contrast, if one were trained in that lab, one would know the rationale for using particular solvents and could experiment with them. The advantage of teaching is that it frees learners from slavishly copying models because they come to understand the rationale for certain steps. This allows them not only to be competent in their domain but also to contribute to it, an aspect of expertise that is emphasized both in Collins and Evans's (2008) notion of contributory expertise, and in Goldman's (2018) CAP definition of expertise. Once you know which parts of the plant processing detoxify it, and which merely make the product taste better, you can skip some steps without endangering your health. But unlike imitation, this requires explicit, verbal instruction. This can provide understanding, which is much harder to obtain through imitative learning alone.

The notion of teacher-as-expert captures something cross-culturally stable about the transmission of expertise in human cultures: humans have been reliant on experts to transmit knowledge and this often occurs in a teaching situation. This does not mean that every exemplar of the novice/expert problem is a novice/teacher situation. Rather, it is useful when one is a novice in *D,* faced with experts in *D,* to regard them as one would a teacher: teachers have some authority, as is the case in the expert-as-authority model, but they do not require total deference or screening off one's own reasons. A learner is sensible if she looks for reasons for why a teacher offers the testimony he or she gives. Accepting what a teacher says without looking for these reasons would be *taqlīd* – uncritical acceptance of testimony (see Section 2).

Some epistemologists (e.g., Pritchard, 2008) have argued that propositional knowledge, even causal propositional knowledge, is distinct from understanding. Allison Hills (2009) proposes that understanding cannot be transmitted to the same extent as propositional knowledge. She gives the specific example of moral understanding and argues that having understanding of a moral proposition p requires more than just knowing that p. Specifically, one should be able to explain why p in one's own words, follow an explanation of why p given by someone else, draw from q the conclusion that p, and so on. Although testimony does not always transmit understanding immediately and directly, teaching, when done properly with a willing learner, results in the transmission of insight (this is a high bar to clear, as it requires both a good teacher and a willing learner).

The model of expert-as-teacher is applicable in many domains. In science, it is exemplified by the research-intensive university, where research helps to inform teaching. In the religious domain, it is especially apt, as many religious experts explicitly have the title "teacher." For example, in Hinduism, Buddhism, Jainism, and Sikhism, gurus (teachers) can help laypeople reach religious insight. In Judaism, the term "rabbi" also means teacher. Rabbis are not priests – they do not have special authority to perform rituals, but they have substantial knowledge of the Jewish law and its traditions that gives them authority to transmit it. The title "teacher" does not mean that these experts always literally teach, but it says something about their contributory expertise: they are able to contribute to laypeople's knowledge by imparting their distinctive knowledge or skills.

5.5 Deciding Whom to Trust: Maimonides on the Talmudic Sages

The model of expert-as-teacher provides some general guidelines on how novices should evaluate teachers. It strikes a balance between the maximal deference of the expert-as-authority model and the pick-and-choose attitude that may be engendered by the expert-as-advisor model. It indicates that we should see experts prima facie as authorities but not screen off our own reasoning. Maimonides provides an insight into how this model might work.

The Jewish medieval philosopher Moses Maimonides (Rabbi Mōšeh bēn-Maymōn, also known by the acronym Rambam, 1138–1204) was born in Córdoba, which had a flourishing Jewish community and culture under Islamic rule, with religious discussions among Christians, Muslims, and Jews, as well as an increasing influence of Aristotelian philosophy. When Córdoba was taken over by the Almohad Caliphate in 1148, Christians and Jews lost their protected status and were offered the choice between conversion, death, or exile. Maimonides's family chose exile and settled in Fez, Morocco, which was also a multicultural and multi-religious city. His *Guide of the Perplexed* (completed in 1190) was ostensibly written for his student Joseph ben Judah, a Jewish physician and poet, who could not integrate philosophy with religious teachings. The *Guide* is a rich resource of philosophical thought, including on the existence and attributes of God (such as his incorporeality), negative theology, and extensive critiques of Christian and Islamic philosophical theology (Seeskin, 2017).

Several parts of the *Guide* deal with the Talmudic sages, or Rabbis (with a capital R). These were Talmudic scholars of the first five centuries CE, whose corpus of writings lies at the basis of the Halakhah, the Jewish law. Traditional Jewish practice is more influenced by the rabbinic interpretations of the Torah than by its original text, hence the importance of these writings. There was, of course, a distinction between the written Torah and the Rabbis' understanding of it. This distinction was formalized in the notion of a dual Torah, consisting of the original written Torah and its interpretation, the oral Torah, which forms part of the Talmud. The Halakhah was necessary because the Pentateuch itself is often brief and lacking in detail. The Rabbis helped to turn those terse formulations into concrete directives for practicing Jews. For example, Leviticus 23:42 states that for the Feast of Tabernacles (*sukkot*), "You shall dwell in booths for seven days. All native Israelites shall dwell in booths." No details are provided about the dimensions and materials of these booths, about whether the directive applies to everyone or whether there are exemptions for those with disabilities, or whether dwelling requires some transfer of one's household items to the booths. There were several techniques for interpretation, including analogical reasoning (look for similar cases where the Pentateuch does provide more detail), exegetical arguments, logical reasoning, and transmitted traditions. Using different techniques led to different interpretations, which is why the Talmud contains so many disagreements (Berger, 1998).

Throughout his works, Maimonides shows tremendous respect for the Talmud. Nevertheless, the Talmudic authors disagreed with one another on several fundamental questions, such as the timing of the Coming of the Messiah. Maimonides disagreed with them on particular topics such as the validity of astrology. He soundly and categorically rejected astrology, deeming it a form of pseudo-expertise. His main reasons for this rejection are that astrology, contrary to astronomy, fails on scientific grounds and that it ascribes to celestial bodies divine or nearly divine powers, which is contrary to

Judaism's commitment to the unity and sovereignty of God. He also saw it as an impediment to free will (Langermann, 2000).

The endorsement of astrology by the sages poses a dilemma for Maimonides. On the one hand, he wants to defer to their epistemic authority; on the other, he wishes to reject astrology. His solution to the dilemma is not to cordon off one's own reasons and views when considering the views of the sages:

> I know that you may search and find sayings of some individual sages in the Talmud and Midrashim whose words appear to maintain that at the moment of a man's birth, the stars will cause such and such to happen to him ... it is not proper to abandon matters of reason that have already been verified by proofs, shake loose of them, and depend on the words of a single one of the sages from whom possibly the matter was hidden ... A man should never cast his reason behind him, for the eyes are set in front, not in back. (Maimonides, 12th century [1972], 472)

If a sage makes a statement that contradicts what has been verified by proofs (Maimonides's prime source of knowledge, reason), then he may be mistaken, or we misinterpret what he writes, or his writing should be interpreted in the context of his time and place. Maimonides makes this more explicit in his *Guide*, where he encourages the reader to think about the historical context in which the sages wrote:

> Do not ask me to show that everything they [the Sages] have said concerning astronomical matters conforms to the way things really are. For at that time mathematics were imperfect. They did not speak about this as transmitters of the dicta of the prophets, but rather because in those times they were men of knowledge in those fields or because they had heard these dicta from the men of knowledge who lived in those times. (Maimonides, 12th century [1963b], part III, chapter 15, 459)

Maimonides encourages the reader to see the sages as experts in religious matters, interpreting the Jewish law and what the prophets have said, but this does not make them experts in all domains, for example, astronomy or astrology. To Maimonides even inexperienced students are not completely powerless in the face of dissenting experts and can use their own reasoning to evaluate the conflicting testimony of religious experts. They can use their own reasons to discard implausible claims, for instance, by thinking about cultural influences/limitations of past experts, resisting halo effects, or understanding reasons for why the experts might be disagreeing.

In this section, I have argued that we can productively think of experts as teachers. Experts help us to obtain understanding of a conceptual space we are trying to learn more about. In the religious domain, it is not uncommon to think of religious experts as teachers (e.g., gurus and rabbis). The advantage of this model is that experts get deference due to their epistemic authority, but that we can still appraise critically what they have to say. Maimonides's approach to the Talmudic sages illustrates how we can treat religious experts: with due respect, but without screening off our own reasons.

6 Why Philosophy Matters to Religious Disagreement

Regulative epistemology aims to shape our doxastic practices, to help us obtain desirable belief outcomes. Throughout this Element, I've been agnostic about what these outcomes could be. Epistemologists have disagreed about what the fundamental epistemic good(s) could be: among others, they have proposed true (accurate) beliefs, knowledge, justified beliefs, warranted beliefs, and understanding. For some authors, such as al-Ghazālī, we should aim for nothing less than religious knowledge. Al-Ghazālī was pessimistic about tradition, sense perception, and reason as sources of knowledge, and he believed that mystical experience was the only secure way to learn about God. However, most people accept a wide range of sources for justification and knowledge. These include perception, memory, reason, and testimony. All of these channels are vulnerable to skeptical worries.

Religious disagreement elicits skeptical worries about whether we can have any religious knowledge at all, and whether we can trust (any) religious experts. Since most of us live in religiously diverse communities, we are confronted with such disagreements on a daily basis. Philosophical argumentation and analysis can make distinctive contributions in the public sphere when religious disagreement occurs. These include arguments in philosophy of religion and analysis of religious disagreements by social epistemologists. Ideally, philosophical reflection should be more than mere post hoc rationalizations of beliefs we already hold; it should genuinely improve our beliefs and the way we form them. Some authors, such as Regina Rini (2017), have expressed skepticism about our ability to alter our individual epistemic practices. She gives the example of fake news, where people reasonably trust the testimony of those who are similar to them and thus are tricked into sharing and endorsing fabricated news stories, often of a highly partisan nature. Others, such as Jonathan Haidt (2001) propose that reasoning (philosophical or otherwise) is largely post hoc rationalization. We reason to affirm beliefs we already hold. This pessimistic picture even seems to hold up for philosophers. In a series of papers, Eric Schwitzgebel and colleagues (see e.g., Schwitzgebel, 2014, for an overview) investigated whether ethicists' behavior is more morally praiseworthy compared to that of other philosophers. Moral self-improvement is an important motivation for ethics (e.g., virtue ethics). If ethics could help us lead a good (ethical) life, we should expect ethicists to behave more ethically than other people. But this is not the case. On a wide range of measures, such as signing up as an organ donor, eating meat, not stealing library books, clearing away trash after talks, ethicists are similar to other philosophers or the population at large. This seems to indicate that what ethicists are doing is post hoc reasoning rather than shaping their ethical beliefs in any way that has an impact on what they are doing.

Nevertheless, small alterations in individual reasoning practices can potentially improve debates in the public sphere. There is an increasing body of empirical research indicating that our reasoning is intimately connected to argumentation, and that reasoning is inherently social (Mercier & Sperber, 2017). Debates about highly polarized and loaded topics tend to be of poor quality, but the quality of the argumentation is improved when conducted in small face-to-face groups with the soft prodding of moderators. For example, Luskin, O'Flynn, Fishkin, & Russell (2014) let parents of school-aged children in a community in Northern Ireland debate the future of local schools. Roman Catholics and Protestants, who until recently were engaged in violent conflict, are polarized about this topic. Nevertheless, the debates proved fruitful and constructive, and citizens left the debates with consensus on some topics. Hugo Mercier and Dan Sperber (2017, chap. 17) discuss the example of the early abolitionist movement as a case where debate about a morally charged topic (slave ownership) resulted in a dramatic shift in policy and attitudes. The abolitionists won their case by pointing out inconsistencies in their opponents' views. For example, those who were pro-slavery argued that slaves were well treated (and certainly better off than they would have been in Africa), because there was an economic incentive to do so. By contrast, William Wilberforce, a British Member of Parliament who lobbied for the abolitionist cause, argued that it was more profitable for slavers to crowd slaves together while being transported, so the argument that economic incentive leads to better treatment did not always hold up. This and other arguments ultimately convinced the majority of British MPs to gradually abolish the slave trade. Reasoning also proves fruitful in changing people's minds about polarized topics such as climate change, with American liberals more likely to accept scientific claims about climate change as human induced compared to conservatives. Michael Ranney and Dav Clark (2016) showed that when participants see short instructional videos that explain the mechanisms of climate change, their acceptance of the scientific climate change consensus was increased, in both liberals and conservatives.

These examples indicate that argumentation works, and that debates can be fruitful in changing attitudes, even those that are highly entrenched. Philosophers of religion often provide expert versions of ordinary religious disagreements, such as about the problem of evil or the epistemic significance of religious revelation (see Section 5). Philosophers have developed elaborate versions of such everyday debates and have carefully considered counterarguments and defenses. Thus, while philosophers of religion are not in a privileged epistemic position about, say, the existence of God, they are experts in articulating reasons and arguments about God's existence and other religious topics. Thus, a better take-up of philosophical arguments about religion in the public sphere can help us to improve discussions among laypeople.

An emerging literature in experimental philosophy indicates that the intuitions of philosophers in a variety of fields, including ethics and epistemology, are quite similar to those of laypeople (e.g., Schwitzgebel & Cushman, 2015). While we can interpret this pessimistically, namely, that there is no such thing as philosophical expertise, the fact that there is nothing inherently philosophical about philosophy is also a good thing. In particular, the claim that philosophers draw on the same sorts of reasoning and resources as ordinary people also means that philosophical knowledge does not require any special defense or justification (Gutting, 2009). This means that we can evaluate philosophical claims the way we evaluate other claims or arguments, by looking at the evidence, the soundness of the argument, and so on. We saw that irrelevant causal factors such as upbringing and education play a role in the religious beliefs we for the most part end up having (Section 2), and that they also play a role in conversions (Section 3). Philosophers of religion are not immune to irrelevant influences. But this is not a problem; we can let diversity work. Given the wide diversity of religious beliefs across cultures, it is important that philosophers of religion engage with a wide range of traditions, not just those found in Christianity in Western cultures. Such arguments can then be used in the public sphere to reason about religious matters. Intellectual diversity and thoughtful debate help communities obtain more justified beliefs.

Acknowledgments

Many thanks to Johan De Smedt, Hugh Burling, Kevin Schilbrack, Neil Van Leeuwen, Matthew Benton, Kate Kirkpatrick, Liam Kofi Bright, and Jonathan Ichikawa Jenkins for their comments to an earlier version of this manuscript. Permission has been granted by the Editor of Philosophia Christi to use material in whole or in part from "Religious Conversion, Transformative Experience, and Disagreement", Philosophia Christi 20 (1), 265–275.

References

Al-Ghazālī, A. H. M. (11th century [1963]). *The incoherence of the philosophers* (S. A. Kamali, Trans.). Lahore: Pakistan Philosophical Congress.

Al-Ghazālī, A. H. M. (ca. 1100 [1952]). *Deliverance from error.* In W. M. Watt (Trans.), *The practice and faith of al-Ghazālī* (pp. 1–359). London: Allen & Unwin.

Alston, W. P. (1991). *Perceiving God. The epistemology of religious experience.* Ithaca, NY: Cornell University Press.

Asiedu, F. B. A. (2001). The limits of Augustine's Personal Authority: The Hermeneutics of Trust in De utilitate credendi. In K. Paffenroth & K. L. Hughes (Eds.), *Augustine and liberal education* (pp. 124–145). Lanham: Rowman & Littlefield.

Augustine. (5th century CE [1961]). *Confessions* (R. S. Pine-Coffin, Trans.). London: Penguin.

Augustine. (5th century [1953]). The usefulness of belief (De utilitate credendi). In J. H. S. Burleigh (Ed.), *Augustine: Earlier writings* (pp. 284–323). Philadelphia: Westminster Press.

Ballantyne, N., & Coffman, E. (2012). Conciliationism and uniqueness. *Australasian Journal of Philosophy, 90,* 657–670.

Barnett, Z. (in press). Belief dependence: How do the numbers count? *Philosophical Studies,* 1–23.

Barrett, J. L. (2004). Why would anyone believe in God? Lanham, MD: AltaMita Press.

Barrett, J. L., Richert, R. A., & Driesenga, A. (2001). God's beliefs versus mother's: The development of nonhuman agent concepts. *Child Development, 72,* 50–65.

Benton, M. A. (2016). Expert opinion and second-hand knowledge. *Philosophy and Phenomenological Research, 92,* 492–508.

Berger, M. (1998). *Rabbinic authority.* Oxford: Oxford University Press.

Bogardus, T. (2013). The problem of contingency for religious belief. *Faith and Philosophy, 30,* 371–392.

Bourget, D., & Chalmers, D. J. (2014). What do philosophers believe? *Philosophical Studies, 170,* 465–500.

Calvin, J. (1559 [1960]). *Institutes of the Christian religion* (F. L. Battles, Trans.). Philadelphia: Westminster Press.

Carel, H., Kidd, I. J., & Pettigrew, R. (2016). Illness as transformative experience. *The Lancet, 388*(10050), 1152–1153.

Christensen, D. (2007). Epistemology of disagreement: The good news. *Philosophical Review, 116*(2), 187–217.

Christensen, D. (2010). Higher-order evidence. *Philosophy and Phenomenological Research, 81*(1), 185–215.

Christensen, D. (2011). Disagreement, question-begging, and epistemic self-criticism. *Philosopher's Imprint, 11*(6), 1–22.

Clark, K. J., & Barrett, J. L. (2010). Reformed epistemology and the cognitive science of religion. *Faith and Philosophy, 27,* 174–189.

Cohen, G. A. (2000). *If you're an egalitarian, how come you're so rich?* Cambridge, MA: Harvard University Press.

Collins, H., & Evans, R. (2008). *Rethinking expertise.* Chicago and London: University of Chicago Press.

Cummins, R. (1998). Reflections on reflective equilibrium. In W. Ramsey & M. DePaul (Eds.), *The role of intuition in philosophy* (pp. 113–127). New York: Rowman & Littlefield.

De Cruz, H. (2018). Religious belief and philosophical views: A qualitative study. *Res Philosophica, 95*(3), 477–504.

De Cruz, H. (2017). Religious disagreement: An empirical study among academic philosophers. *Episteme, 14,* 71–87.

De Cruz, H., & De Smedt, J. (2015). A natural history of natural theology. *The cognitive science of theology and philosophy of religion.* Cambridge, MA: MIT Press.

De Cruz, H., & De Smedt, J. (2013). Reformed and evolutionary epistemology and the noetic effects of sin. *International Journal for Philosophy of Religion, 74*(1), 49–66.

Dellsén, F. (2018). When expert disagreement supports the consensus. *Australasian Journal of Philosophy, 96,* 142–156.

Dixon, R. D., Lowery, R. C., & Jones, L. P. (1992). The fact and form of born-again religious conversions and sociopolitical conservatism. *Review of Religious Research, 34,* 117–131.

Douven, I. (2010). Simulating peer disagreements. *Studies in History and Philosophy of Science A, 41,* 148–157.

Draper, P., & Nichols, R. (2013). Diagnosing cognitive biases in philosophy of religion. *The Monist, 96,* 420–444.

Easwaran, K., Fenton-Glynn, L., Hitchcock, C., & Velasco, J. D. (2016). Updating on the credences of others: Disagreement, agreement, and synergy. *Philosophers' Imprint, 16*(11), 1–39.

Ecklund, E. H., & Scheitle, C. P. (2007). Religion among academic scientists: Distinctions, disciplines, and demographics. *Social Problems, 54*(2), 289–307.

Edwards, J. (1821). *A treatise concerning religious affections, in three parts.* Philadelphia: James Crissy.

Elga, A. (2007). Reflection and disagreement. *Noûs, 41,* 478–502.

Feldman, R. (2007). Reasonable religious disagreements. In L. Anthony (Ed.), *Philosophers without gods* (pp. 194–214). Oxford: Oxford University Press.

Frank, R. M. (1994). *Al-Ghazālī and the Ash'arite school.* Durham and London: Duke University Press.

Fricker, L. (2014). Epistemic trust in oneself and others – An argument from analogy? In L. Callahan & T. O'Connor (Eds.), *Religious faith and intellectual virtue* (pp. 174–203). Oxford: Oxford University Press.

Fridland, E. (in press). Do as I say and as I do: Imitation, pedagogy and cumulative culture. *Mind and Language.*

Gauchat, G. (2012). Politicization of science in the public sphere: A study of public trust in the United States, 1974 to 2010. *American Sociological Review, 77,* 167–187.

Gellman, J. (1997). *Experience of God and the rationality of theistic belief.* Ithaca and London: Cornell University Press.

Gellman, J. (1992). A new look at the problem of evil. *Faith and Philosophy, 9*(2), 210–216.

Goldman, A. I. (2001). Experts: Which ones should you trust? *Philosophy and Phenomenological Research, 63,* 85–110.

Goldman, A. I. (2018). Expertise. *Topoi, 37,* 3–10.

Gould, S. J. (2001). Nonoverlapping magisteria. In R. Pennock (Ed.), *Intelligent design creationism and its critics. Philosophical, theological, and scientific perspectives* (pp. 737–749). Cambridge, MA: MIT Press.

Griffel, F. (2005). *Taqlīd* of the philosophers: al-Ghazālī's initial accusation in his *tahāfut.* In S. Günther (Ed.), *Ideas, images, and methods of portrayal: Insights into classical Arabic literature and Islam.* Leiden and Boston: Brill.

Griffel, F. (2017). Al-Ghazālī's Incoherence of the philosophers. In K. El-Rouayheb & S. Schmidtke (Eds.), *The Oxford handbook of Islamic philosophy* (pp. 191–200). Oxford: Oxford University Press.

Gross, N., & Simmons, S. (2009). The religiosity of American college and university professors. *Sociology of Religion, 70,* 101–129.

Guthrie, S. E. (1993). *Faces in the clouds. A new theory of religion.* New York & Oxford: Oxford University Press.

Gutting, G. (1982). *Religious belief and religious skepticism.* Notre Dame, IN: University of Notre Dame Press.

Gutting, G. (2009). *What philosophers know: Case studies in recent analytic philosophy.* Cambridge: Cambridge University Press.

Haidt, J. (2001). The emotional dog and its rational tail: A social intuitionist approach to moral judgment. *Psychological Review, 108*, 814–834.

Harris, P. L., & Corriveau, K. H. (2011). Young children's selective trust in informants. *Philosophical Transactions of the Royal Society B, 366*, 1179–1187.

Heiphetz, L., Spelke, E. S., Harris, P. L., & Banaji, M. R. (2013). The development of reasoning about beliefs: Fact, preference, and ideology. *Journal of Experimental Social Psychology, 49*, 559–565.

Hick, J. (1988). God and the universe of faiths. *Essays in the philosophy of religion*. London: Macmillan.

Hills, A. (2009). Moral testimony and moral epistemology. *Ethics, 120*, 94–127.

Hume, D. (1757). The natural history of religion. In *Four dissertations* (pp. 1–117). London: A. Millar.

James, W. (1902). *The varieties of religious experience. A study in human nature*. New York: Longmans, Green, and Co.

Janzen, J. (1978). *The quest for therapy in Lower Zaire*. Berkeley: University of California Press.

Kelemen, D. (2004). Are children "intuitive theists"? Reasoning about purpose and design in nature. *Psychological Science, 15*, 295–301.

Kelley, J., & De Graaf, N. D. (1997). National context, parental socialization, and religious belief: Results from 15 nations. *American Sociological Review, 62*, 639–659.

Kelly, T. (2011). *Consensus gentium*: Reflections on the 'common consent' argument for the existence of God. In K. J. Clark & R. J. VanArragon (Eds.), *Evidence and religious belief* (pp. 135–156). Oxford: Oxford University Press.

King, N. L. (2012). Disagreement: What's the problem? Or a good peer is hard to find. *Philosophy and Phenomenological Research, 85*, 249–272.

King, P., & Ballantyne, N. (2009). Augustine on testimony. *Canadian Journal of Philosophy, 39*(2), 195–214.

Kitcher, P. (1990). The division of cognitive labor. *Journal of Philosophy, 87*, 5–22.

Kox, W., Meeus, W., & Hart, H. (1991). Religious conversion of adolescents: Testing the Lofland and Stark model of religious conversion. *Sociological Analysis, 52*(3), 227–240.

Lackey, J. (2010). What should we do when we disagree? In T. Gendler & J. Hawthorne (Eds.), *Oxford studies in epistemology* (Vol. *3*, pp. 274–293). Oxford: Oxford University Press.

Lackey, J. (2011). Assertion and isolated second-hand knowledge. In J. Brown & H. Cappelen (Eds.), *Assertion: New philosophical essays* (pp. 251–275). Oxford: Oxford University Press.

Lackey, J. (2018). Experts and peer disagreement. In M. Benton, J. Hawthorne, & D. Rabinowitz (Eds.), *Knowledge, belief, and God: New insights in religious epistemology* (pp. 228–245). Oxford: Oxford University Press.

Lakhdar, M., Vinsonneau, G., Apter, M. J., & Mullet, E. (2007). Conversion to Islam among French adolescents and adults: A systematic inventory of motives. *International Journal for the Psychology of Religion, 17*(1), 1–15.

Lane, J. D., Wellman, H. M., & Gelman, S. A. (2013). Informants' traits weigh heavily in young children's trust in testimony and in their epistemic inferences. *Child Development, 84*, 1253–1268.

Langermann, Y. T. (2000). Maimonides' repudiation of astrology. In R. S. Cohen & H. Levine (Eds.), *A Maimonides reader* (pp. 131–157). Dordrecht: Springer.

Legare, C. H. (2017). Cumulative cultural learning: Development and diversity. *Proceedings of the National Academy of Sciences, 114*(30), 7877–7883.

Levinstein, B. A. (2015). With all due respect: The macro-epistemology of disagreement. *Philosopher's Imprint, 15*(13), 1–20.

Levy, N. (2017). Religious beliefs are factual beliefs: Content does not correlate with context sensitivity. *Cognition, 161*, 109–116.

Levy, N. (in press). Due deference to denialism: Explaining ordinary people's rejection of established scientific findings. *Synthese*, 1–15.

Lindeman, M., Svedholm-Häkkinen, A. M., & Lipsanen, J. (2015). Ontological confusions but not mentalizing abilities predict religious belief, paranormal belief, and belief in supernatural purpose. *Cognition, 134*, 63–76.

Littlejohn, C. (2013). Disagreement and defeat. In D. E. Machuca (Ed.), *Disagreement and skepticism* (pp. 169–192). London and New York: Routledge.

Lofland, J., & Stark, R. (1965). Becoming a world-saver: A theory of conversion to a deviant perspective. *American Sociological Review, 30*, 862–875.

Longino, H. E. (1991). Multiplying subjects and the diffusion of power. *Journal of Philosophy, 88*, 666–674.

Luhrmann, T. M. (2006). The art of hearing God: Absorption, dissociation, and contemporary American spirituality. *Spiritus: A Journal of Christian Spirituality, 5*, 133–157.

Luhrmann, T. M. (2012a). A hyperreal God and modern belief. *Current Anthropology, 53*, 371–395.

Luhrmann, T. M. (2012b). *When God talks back. Understanding the American Evangelical relationship with God*. New York: Vintage.

Luskin, R. C., O'Flynn, I., Fishkin, J. S., & Russell, D. (2014). Deliberating across deep divides. *Political Studies*, *62*(1), 116–135.

Maimonides, M. (12th century [1963a]). *The guide of the perplexed* (Vol. 1; S. Pines, Trans.). Chicago: University of Chicago Press.

Maimonides, M. (12th century [1963b]). *The guide of the perplexed* (Vol. 2; S. Pines, Trans.). Chicago: University of Chicago Press.

Maimonides, M. (12th century [1972]). Letter on astrology. In I. Twersky (Ed.), *A Maimonides reader* (pp. 463–473). Springfield, NJ: Behrman House.

Matheson, J. (2009). Conciliatory views of disagreement and higher-order evidence. *Episteme*, *6*(3), 269–279.

Mercier, H., & Sperber, D. (2017). *The enigma of reason*. Cambridge, MA: Harvard University Press.

Mill, J. S. (1859). *On liberty*. London: John W. Parker and Son.

Mill, J. S. (1874). *Three essays on religion*. London: Henry Holt and Co.

Nagel, J. (2012). Intuitions and experiments: A defense of the case method in epistemology. *Philosophy and Phenomenological Research*, *85*, 495–527.

Nielsen, M., Mushin, I., Tomaselli, K., & Whiten, A. (2014). Where culture takes hold: "Overimitation" and its flexible deployment in Western, Aboriginal, and Bushmen children. *Child Development*, *85*, 2169–2184.

Norenzayan, A., Gervais, W. M., & Trzesniewski, K. H. (2012). Mentalizing deficits constrain belief in a personal god. *PLoS ONE*, *7*, e36880.

Paloutzian, R. F., Richardson, J. T., & Rambo, L. R. (1999). Religious conversion and personality change. *Journal of Personality*, 67(6), 1047–1079.

Pasnau, R. (2015). Disagreement and the value of self-trust. *Philosophical Studies*, *172*(9), 2315–2339.

Paul, L. A. (2014). *Transformative experience*. Oxford: Oxford University Press.

Peels, R. (2015). Believing at will is possible. *Australasian Journal of Philosophy*, *93*, 524–541.

Pettigrew, R. (2016). Jamesian epistemology formalised: An explication of "the will to believe." *Episteme*, *13*, 253–268.

Plantinga, A. (2000). *Warranted Christian belief*. New York: Oxford University Press.

Pollock, J. L. (1987). Defeasible reasoning. *Cognitive Science*, *11*, 481–518.

Potter, K. (2013). Religious disagreement: Internal and external. *International Journal for Philosophy of Religion*, *74*, 21–31.

Pritchard, D. (2008). Knowing the answer, understanding, and epistemic value. *Grazer Philosophische Studien*, *77*(1), 325–339.

Pronin, E., Lin, D. Y., & Ross, L. (2002). The bias blind spot: Perceptions of bias in self versus others. *Personality and Social Psychology Bulletin*, *28*(3), 369–381.

Ranney, M. A., & Clark, D. (2016). Climate change conceptual change: Scientific information can transform attitudes. *Topics in Cognitive Science*, *8*(1), 49–75.

Reid, J. (2015). The common consent argument from Herbert to Hume. *Journal of the History of Philosophy*, *53*, 401–433.

Rini, R. (2017). Fake news and partisan epistemology. *Kennedy Institute of Ethics Journal*, *27*(2), E43–E64.

Roberts, R. C., & Wood, W. J. (2007). *Intellectual virtues: An essay in regulative epistemology*. Oxford: Oxford University Press.

Rollins, J. (2015). Beliefs and testimony as social evidence: Epistemic egoism, epistemic universalism, and common consent arguments. *Philosophy Compass*, *10*, 78–90.

Rowe, W. L. (1979). The problem of evil and some varieties of atheism. *American Philosophical Quarterly*, *16*, 335–341.

Schoenfield, M. (2014). Permission to believe: Why permissivism is true and what it tells us about irrelevant influences on belief. *Noûs*, *48*, 193–218.

Schwitzgebel, E. (2014). The moral behavior of ethicists and the role of the philosopher. In C. Luetge, H. Rusch, & M. Uhl (Eds.), *Experimental ethics: Toward an empirical moral philosophy* (pp. 59–64). Dordrecht: Springer.

Schwitzgebel, E., & Cushman, F. (2015). Philosophers' biased judgments persist despite training, expertise and reflection. *Cognition*, *141*, 127–137.

Seeskin, K. (2017). Maimonides. *Stanford Encyclopedia of Philosophy*, retrieved September 21, 2017, from https://plato.stanford.edu/archives/spr2017/entries/maimonides/

Shea, N. (2009). Imitation as an inheritance system. *Philosophical Transactions of the Royal Society of London B: Biological Sciences*, *364*, 2429–2443.

Shtulman, A. (2013). Epistemic similarities between students' scientific and supernatural beliefs. *Journal of Educational Psychology*, *105*, 199–212.

Simpson, R. M. (2017). Permissivism and the arbitrariness objection. *Episteme*, 14(4)519–538.

Smith, J. (1902). History of the Church of Jesus Christ of the Latter-Day Saints. *Period I: History of Joseph Smith, the prophet, by himself* (Vol. 1). Salt Lake City: Deseret News.

Sperber, D., Clément, F., Heintz, C., Mascaro, O., Mercier, H., Origgi, G., & Wilson, D. (2010). Epistemic vigilance. *Mind and Language*, *25*, 359–393.

Stanford, K. (2006). *Exceeding our grasp: Science, history, and the problem of unconceived alternatives*. New York: Oxford University Press.

Stroud, S. (2006). Epistemic partiality in friendship. *Ethics*, *116*, 498–524.

Swinburne, R. (2004). *The existence of God* (6th ed.). Oxford: Clarendon Press.

Taves, A. (2016). *Revelatory events. Three case studies of the emergence of new spiritual paths*. Princeton, NJ: Princeton University Press.

Teresa of Ávila. (1577 [1921]). The interior castle or the mansions. www.ccel.org/ccel/teresa/castle2.pdf.

Van Inwagen, P. (1996). It is wrong, everywhere, always, for anyone, to believe anything upon insufficient evidence. In J. Jordan & D. Howard-Snyder (Eds.), *Faith, freedom and rationality* (pp. 137–154). Savage, MD: Rowman and Littlefield.

Van Leeuwen, N. (2014). Religious credence is not factual belief. *Cognition*, *133*, 698–715.

Van Leeuwen, N. & van Elk, M. (in press). Seeking the supernatural: The interactive religious experience model. *Religion, Brain and Behavior*.

Vavova, K. (2018). Irrelevant influences. *Philosophy and Phenomenological Research*, *96*(1), 134–152.

Wedgwood, R. (2007). *The nature of normativity*. Oxford: Oxford University Press.

Wettstein, H. (2012). *The significance of religious experience*. New York: Oxford University Press.

White, R. (2014). Evidence cannot be permissive. In M. Steup, J. Turri, & E. Sosa (Eds.), *Contemporary debates in epistemology* (pp. 312–323). Oxford: Oxford University Press.

Whiten, A., Allan, G., Devlin, S., Kseib, N., Raw, N., & McGuigan, N. (2016). Social learning in the real-world: 'Over-imitation' occurs in both children and adults unaware of participation in an experiment and independently of social interaction. *PloS One*, *11*(7), e0159920.

Wolterstorff, N. (1996). *John Locke and the ethics of belief*. Cambridge: Cambridge University Press.

Worrall, J. (2004). Science discredits religion. In M. L. Peterson & R. J. VanArragon (Eds.), *Contemporary debates in philosophy of religion* (pp. 59–72). Malden, MA: Blackwell.

Zagzebski, L. (2011). Epistemic self-trust and the *Consensus Gentium* argument. In K. J. Clark & R. J. VanArragon (Eds.), *Evidence and religious belief* (pp. 22–36). Oxford: Oxford University Press.

Zagzebski, L. (2012). *Epistemic authority: A theory of trust, authority, and autonomy in belief*. Oxford: Oxford University Press.

Zuckerman, P. (2007). Atheism. Contemporary numbers and patterns. In M. Martin (Ed.), *The Cambridge companion to atheism* (pp. 47–65). Cambridge: Cambridge University Press.

Cambridge Elements ☰

Philosophy of Religion

Yujin Nagasawa
University of Birmingham

Yujin Nagasawa is Professor of Philosophy and Co-Director of the John Hick Centre for Philosophy of Religion at the University of Birmingham. He is currently President of the British Society for the Philosophy of Religion. He is a member of the Editorial Board of *Religious Studies*, the *International Journal for Philosophy of Religion* and *Philosophy Compass*.

About the series

This Cambridge Elements series provides concise and structured introductions to all the central topics in the philosophy of religion. It offers balanced, comprehensive coverage of multiple perspectives in the philosophy of religion. Contributors to the series are cutting-edge researchers who approach central issues in the philosophy of religion. Each provides a reliable resource for academic readers and develops new ideas and arguments from a unique viewpoint.

Cambridge Elements ☰

Philosophy of Religion

Elements in the series